INSTANT
CONTAINER
GARDENS

Where to buy "Instant Container Gardens" book:

The book is available through many garden centers and book sellers. It is also available through www.kinsmangarden.com and www.amazon.com. To locate your nearest source or place an order with the publisher, contact us at:
Color Garden Publishing
1353 Riverstone Parkway, Canton, GA 30114
Phone: 770-704-6437   Fax: 770-720-9719
Web site: www.easygardencolor.com
Email: info@easygardencolor.com

Where to buy "Instant Container" products:

From garden centers: Go to www.sideplanting.com to find a list of garden centers near you. This is a great choice because you can pick up the plants and potting mix at the same time.
 Online: Go to www.kinsmangarden.com for retail and www.kinsmanwholesale.com for wholesale.
 Phone: 1-800-733-4146 for retail orders or 1-800-733-5613 for wholesale orders.

Credits:

Author: Pamela Crawford
Research Assistant: Barbara Hadsell
Cover Design and Graphic Design Assistance: Elaine Weber Designs, Inc. (www.ewdlogos.com)
Proofreader: Barbara Iderosa, Best Editing Service, Wellington, Florida
Container Design: Pamela Crawford, Barbara Hadsell
Landscape Design: Pamela Crawford
Photography: All photos by Pamela Crawford except for:
 Pages 10-11, 18-19, and 22-23: Marvin Cargle
 Pages 16-19: Scott McNees
 All products in chapter 1, window box on page 72: Kinsman Company
 Torenia photos on page 39, 82, and 89, *Scaevola* 'Whirlwind White' on page 39, black mondo on pages 91 and 154, *Schizanthus* on page 114 and 154, Sweet potato, and petunias on page 82-83, lobelia on page 154, vinca vine on page 154: Proven Winners
 Giant coleus on page 34: Ball Seed Company
 Printing: Asianprinting.com, Korea

Published by Color Garden, Inc., Canton, GA. First printing, 2007. Second printing, 2008. Third printing, 2009.
Library of Congress Catalog Card Number pending

ISBN number: 0-9712220-5-3

Contents

About the Author

Above: This was one of the baskets I made before doing the research that led to this book. I planted the top only, so quite a bit of the sides showed. Boring, at best!

Above: Baskets like this gorgeous specimen were all over Victoria, Canada. They were planted in the sides as well as the tops.

Above: My first attempt at side planting looked just awful!

I began gardening at age three with my English mother, who made gardening look effortless. I was so excited when I moved into my first house – more so about the garden than about the interior. I planned a gorgeous garden filled with color.

The next few years brought more blunders than blooms as I made every gardening mistake in the book! These early errors started a three-decade saga of learning everything I could about gardening, particularly regarding how to make gardening easier. I received a Master's Degree in Landscape Architecture, then started a nursery and garden design business. While designing 1500 gardens, I also started my own trial gardens (on the eight acres where I lived and worked) to determine which plants gave the best performances with the least amount of care.

After writing several landscaping books, I turned my attention to container gardening with the intention of writing a book on the subject. Although I had extensive experience with container gardening, I didn't feel my experience had resulted in as much impact as I wanted from container gardens.

So, I hit the road. I traveled to New York, Long Island, the Hamptons, Chicago, Vail, Seattle, Beverly Hills, San Francisco, Victoria, Vancouver, Philadelphia, Florida, and Georgia to see what I could find.

I hit the jackpot! Many public plantings in these areas were loaded with gorgeous container gardens. The theme parks - particularly Disney World, Universal Studios, and Busch Gardens - were bursting with fabulous examples.

My favorite container gardens were the huge, hanging baskets I saw in many, public locations. I was bound and determined to figure out how to make them so I could create them myself.

I thoroughly researched these baskets and discovered they were planted through the sides as well as in the tops. Wire baskets were lined with spaghnum moss, and seedlings were threaded through the sides.

My first attempt at this method is pictured at left. It was a disaster! Not only did it take over an hour to stuff each basket with spaghnum moss, but it also held so much water that the stems of the seedlings rotted. All the plants died! And, it looked just awful – a situation made worse by its visible location right outside my front door. Who would want something that looks like this hanging outside their front door for two months until it filled out?

This method would obviously not work for home gardeners. People were telling me that they didn't have time to grow seedlings. They wanted fast, instant, and easy.

Above: This basket was planted in the top only. It will take months for the plants to cover the sides, which is usually the goal with hanging baskets.

Above: This basket was planted in the top and through the sides. It looked good instantly! My problem in the early days was how to get the plants through the sides in a reasonable amount of time.

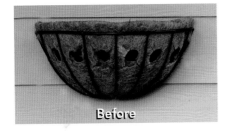

Before

After

Above: Instant containers are designed to make side planting easy. The holes are pre-cut in the sides so that the root balls are easily and quickly inserted.

Once I discovered that hanging baskets looked best with the sides covered and that people wanted an instant look, my next challenge was to figure out how to do that. I needed to get large plants through the sides, but there were no products I could find that allowed this.

So, I tried cutting wires out of baskets to allow large rootballs though and cutting holes in coco fiber liners to hold the whole thing together. It took forever! Finally, I found some baskets that had widely-spaced wires to accommodate plants with 4" root balls. I lined these with loose coco-fiber, which resembles hay, and planted away.

My first container garden book (*Container Gardens for Florida*) included this method. Many of my readers complained that they couldn't find the baskets or coco fiber. Others told me it took too long to plant one (45 minutes). Others said that the baskets they found were too large – they couldn't lift them.

So, I still needed many improvements. I designed containers and liners that would simplify this whole planting process. The containers feature pre-cut holes in the coco fiber liners that make planting fast and easy. I also included a range of sizes, from small and light to large and heavy. Finally! It only took me about 10 years to figure it out!

Kinsman Company agreed to make and distribute the new baskets. I was happy dealing with Kinsman because I had extensively tested their products for many years. Their hanging baskets lasted the longest time outdoors. After 10 years outside in Florida, they showed no rust at all!

Kinsman is now making the whole line. Consumers can easily find them at many garden centers (see www.sideplanting.com), or online (www.kinsmangarden.com) or on the phone (1-800-733-4146 for retail and 1-800-733-5613 for wholesale). Since my most common complaint from my readers is that they can't find whatever product I'm writing about, I am thrilled that Kinsman is making it so easy for everyone.

Our instant container line is much more than just hanging baskets. It features wall planters, window boxes, and basic baskets. The basic baskets can be hung like a hanging basket or mounted on columns. The columns can be placed in the garden (on metal stakes) or put on stands for the patio.

I am especially excited about the baskets on columns. They add instant impact to a garden, which is hard to do. They also put the flowers at eye level, where it is easy both to see and to take care of them!

Technical Details

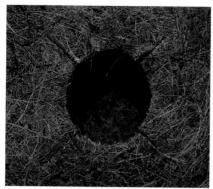

Above: Holes feature slits on the sides.

Center pin

Clips

Above: Mounting the basket to the column is fast, easy, and secure. Line up the hole in the basket with the center pin on the column...

and twist the basket so that its wires are firmly fixed on the clips.

Sizing of Holes

✿ We tried holes from 1" to 2.5" in diameter to discover the best possible size. The 1.7" size is far and above the best choice for 3" to 4.5" root balls. Smaller sizes tear up the larger root balls, and larger ones allow the root balls to fall out. We also tried many different sizes of slits, with the 1" performing the best.

Potting Mix Leakage

Expect some potting mix to escape if you plant with dry potting mix.

✿ After you place the root balls, you will see a small, open space. We first put loose coco fiber in these spaces, so no soil could escape. Then, we tried planting without the loose coco fiber, and the results were great – we lost very little potting mix, and the plants performed beautifully.

✿ To minimize potting mix leakage, firm the dry potting mix slightly with your hand (in the area of the hole on the outside of the container) after planting, and expect a small amount of mix to escape, but nothing significant. The roots grow so quickly in these containers that the soil stabilizes quickly.

✿ If you wet the potting mix first, you minimize the initial mix leakage.

✿ If the containers are placed over hardscape (sidewalks, decks, etc.), expect to sweep up occasionally – just like you would if your container gardens dropped flowers or leaves.

Plants

Not all plants survive side planting.

✿ Some plants like side planting and some don't. We tested thousands of plants to find out which did and which didn't. For example, all the fuchsias died quickly, as did the marigolds. Coleus, begonias, and impatiens thrived. Check Chapters 2 and 8 for this information before planting. These references include test results of many different plant species.

Proper Column Mounting

We tested many different mechanisms for keeping the basket on the column. The large baskets are heavy and need to be mounted properly. We first tried smaller disks, but the pots fell off. The 9" disk is perfect. Our containers went through three direct hits from hurricanes, and stood tall on their columns, which had the proper size disks!

Trial Details

Six Thousand Plants Tested in Three States

We planted over 6000 plants in side-planted containers during our trial period. Our trials took place in south Florida, Georgia, and New Hampshire. The growing conditions varied greatly in these three areas, which gave us a wonderful range of environments to experience.

Planting the top of an instant container is the same as planting any other container. Most plants do just fine. Not so for the sides. Some plants like it and some don't. Read about the winners and losers in Chapter 1.

These trials also gave us the opportunity to grow each basket for its entire lifespan – rather than just getting it ready for a photo. We give you the details of how each container did based on our extensive experience. See Chapters 3, 4, and 5 for this information (pages 46-115).

How Do these Containers Hold Water?

Our initial trials of the instant containers were in the fall, winter, and spring in southeast Florida and in the summer in New Hampshire. The temperatures seldom hit more than 90 degrees in these areas during our trial seasons. Most of the containers were watered by drip irrigation or ground sprinklers. When they were first planted, we watered them about every three days in sun, every five days in shade. When they were fully grown, we watered them about every other day in sun and every three to four days in shade.

Our Georgia (near Atlanta) trials followed. These offered much more of a challenge because we were determined to find out if these containers were a viable option in hotter conditions, like a Georgia summer. Since we wanted to know exactly how many times these containers would need water, we used no automatic methods at all – the containers were hand-watered.

When the June temperatures hit 97 degrees, we were quite concerned that the porous coco fiber sides of the containers would inhibit the water-holding capacity of the container – we even had visions of watering four or five times a day to keep the container alive! Luckily, that was not the case. We watered them, at the most, once a day if they were planted in sun. The shade containers NEVER needed watering more than once every three days.

In areas that are hotter than Atlanta (e.g. Houston), July and August may be a challenging month for almost any container planted in full sun – especially if it is in a windy situation or against a white wall. But these super-hot areas have long growing seasons, so spring and fall would be easier times for container gardening in sun.

If you plan on having a lot of these containers, try an automatic watering system. Drip systems are getting better and better. Check with your local garden center, home improvement store, or irrigation company.

Thank You

Michele Kinsman *Graham Kinsman*

Barbara Hadsell *Elaine Golob Weber*

I wrote this book because I was able to find a great company to make these containers. Working with a business scared me because of concern that they would be much more concerned about speed than quality. Not so for Kinsman. They worked closely with me for as long as it took to get these containers right.

The window boxes are a great example. My original designs were more like hayracks, with fronts that curved inward instead of straight down. The inward curve blocked the light from the side plants. At the last minute, I told Graham Kinsman (the owner) that I had a great, new idea for the window boxes – to make them box-shaped so light would be more available for the sides. The new shape also allowed for more soil, so the plants would grow larger, without as much water. And, they featured a flat bottom so they could be easily transported in a trunk filled with flowers from the garden center. He immediately agreed to the changes, which cost him time and money.

Graham and his wife, Michele worked tirelessly with me for over a year to make this book and these wonderful products available to you.

I also want to thank Barbara Hadsell, my assistant. Barbara tested the plants in New Hampshire as well as Florida. She also gave lots of ideas for our Georgia trial gardens. In addition, Barbara gave lectures and workshops on container gardening and set up trade shows to spread the word of our latest ideas. She is consistently energetic, smart, and tireless!

Elaine Weber, the graphic designer, worked enthusiastically with me on some very tight deadlines. She showed great patience with my last-minute requests.

A Word to Garden Centers

Above: Customers would love to have all the plants for this container displayed together, so that it is easy for them to shop.

Thank you to the many garden centers who are stocking these containers. You are making my work possible!

I am receiving many emails from consumers who want the plants put together as a package for these containers. Buy lots of different coleus, along with wax begonias in 18-packs that can be pulled apart into 6-packs. Three 6-packs are enough side and edge plants for the 14" basic basket (the best-seller), the 24", 30", and 36" window box, and the 16" and 20" wall planters. Display them with one basket empty and the same basket full next to it, with the plants nearby.

Consumers also appreciate a planting service. Set up a potting shed so that your customers can take home finished baskets. Plant them during business hours so that customers can see the process.

USDA Plant Hardiness Map

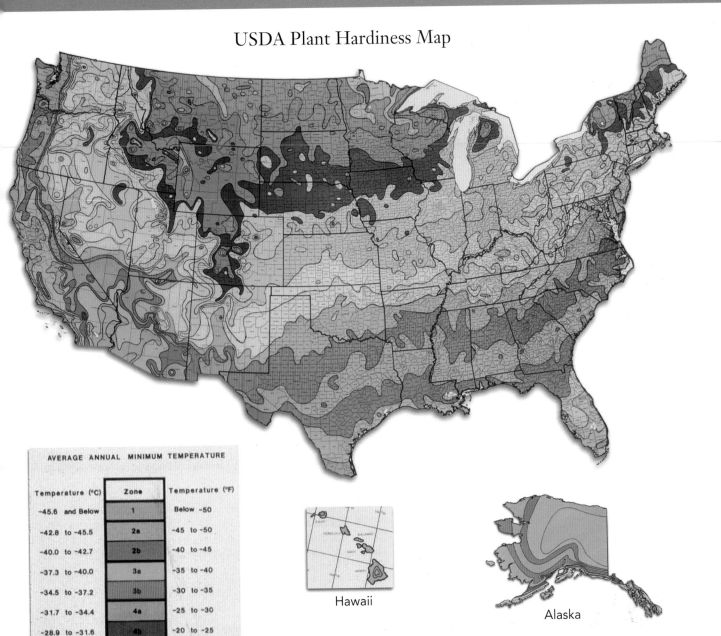

AVERAGE ANNUAL MINIMUM TEMPERATURE

Temperature (°C)	Zone	Temperature (°F)
-45.6 and Below	1	Below -50
-42.8 to -45.5	2a	-45 to -50
-40.0 to -42.7	2b	-40 to -45
-37.3 to -40.0	3a	-35 to -40
-34.5 to -37.2	3b	-30 to -35
-31.7 to -34.4	4a	-25 to -30
-28.9 to -31.6	4b	-20 to -25
-26.2 to -28.8	5a	-15 to -20
-23.4 to -26.1	5b	-10 to -15
-20.6 to -23.3	6a	-5 to -10
-17.8 to -20.5	6b	0 to -5
-15.0 to -17.7	7a	5 to 0
-12.3 to -15.0	7b	10 to 5
-9.5 to -12.2	8a	15 to 10
-6.7 to -9.4	8b	20 to 15
-3.9 to -6.6	9a	25 to 20
-1.2 to -3.8	9b	30 to 25
1.6 to -1.1	10a	35 to 30
4.4 to 1.7	10b	40 to 35
4.5 and Above	11	40 and Above

Hawaii

Alaska

The country is divided into zones based on minimum temperatures. Plants are classified by these zone numbers to determine where they can grow based on the lowest temperature they can take.

USDA Miscellaneous Publication No. 1475. Issued January 1990. Authored by Henry M. Cathey while Director, U.S. National Arboretum.

Edited, formatted and prepared for the US National Arboretum web site by Ramon Jordan, March 1998 & Revised March 2001 U.S. National Arboretum, Agricultural Research Service, U.S. Department of Agriculture, Washington, DC 20002 ** Special thanks to Jody Stuart and Scott Bauer, ARS Information Staff

Chapter 1

Materials, Planting, and Maintenance

Skim this chapter before planting your first container. It will save you a lot of time, money, and trouble – and make instant container gardening a lot easier for you.

Planting these containers is quite easy. I included many more steps than are shown on the product labels – maybe too much! But you will know everything you ever wanted to know about planting these unique containers!

Three common mistakes in container gardening:

❁ Wrong potting mix

❁ Fertilizer mis-use

❁ Incorrect watering

See this chapter for easy instructions on these key areas.

Left: Planting a 14" basic basket. It takes only about ten minutes!

Above: Fertilizing with a good, slow-release product.

Baskets

Watch Pamela plant these containers, as well as install columns on her
THREE-MINUTE VIDEO CLIPS
Check it out at **www.sideplanting.com**

Basic Basket Planters WITH ATTACHED LINERS*
For use as Hanging Planters or on Columns or Stands
Supplied with removable clip-on chains

14" SINGLE BASKET PLANTER
14" diameter x 7" deep holds 8 side plants, 8 top edge plants and 1 - 6" or 3 - 4.5" centerpiece plants
Item #ZGBS14

16" SINGLE BASKET PLANTER
16" diameter x 7" deep holds 12 side plants, 12 top edge plants and one 6" or gallon size centerpiece plant
Item #ZGBS16

16" DOUBLE BASKET PLANTER
16" diameter x 11" deep holds 18 side plants, 12 top edge plants and from 1 to 3 - 6" or gallon size centerpiece plants
Item #ZGBD16

20" DOUBLE BASKET PLANTER
20" diameter x 11" deep holds 21 side plants, 14 top edge plants and three 6" or gallon size centerpiece plants
Item #ZGBD20

Imperial Planters WITH ATTACHED LINERS*
For use as Hanging Planters Only

16" SINGLE IMPERIAL PLANTER
16" diameter x 7.5" deep x 24" overall height holds 12 side plants, 12 top edge plants and from 1 to 3 - 6" or gallon size centerpiece plants
Item #ZGBD20

16" DOUBLE IMPERIAL PLANTER
16" diameter x 11.5" deep x 29" overall height holds 18 side plants, 12 top edge plants and from 1 to 3 - 6" or gallon size centerpiece plants
Item #ZGBD20

Replacement liners for all baskets are sold separately.

Swivlit Basket Ring
For use on Small, Single Basket Planters

Nylon hanging basket swivel joint lets you rotate your hanging baskets easily for even growth, without taking them off the hook. Heavy duty, can take loads up to 55 lbs. which works for the 14 and 16 inch single basket planters but none of the double basket planters.
Item #SW1V-2 (2 per pack)

Swivel Hook
For use on Large, Double Basket Planters

This hook is ideal for the large, 16" and 20" double baskets, including the Imperial planter. Look for it at your local home improvement store.

* Patent pending

NOTE: Use plants with rootballs that measure from 3" to 4.5"wide for the sides and edge.

For product sources, see page 15.

Border Columns
For use in Borders, Lawns, and Flower Beds

Border Column Kits include 18" ground spike, 9" dia. steel disk and choice of 24", 30", 36", 42" or 48" height column.

24" Border Column Kit Item #ZGBC24
30" Border Column Kit Item #ZGBC30
36" Border Column Kit Item #ZGBC36
42" Border Column Kit Item #ZGBC42
48" Border Column Kit Item #ZGBC48

Individual components are available separately.

Steel disk with gripping clips and central locator pin

Square black wooden column, available in five heights

18" steel ground spike

Components for Border Columns

The separate availability of these components means you can purchase 4" by 4" columns of any desired lengths and paint or stain them any color.

9" Disk with Gripping Clips
Item #Z9DISK

18" Ground Spike
Item #Z18GSP

Patio Stand

For use with all Baskets Except the Imperials

Features adjustable column providing heights of 16" to 27" (to the bottom of the basket). Shown with a 14" basic basket.

Item #ZGBC24

Patio Stand with Basket

Includes 14" or 16" Basket With a Stand

Display stand on a patio, as shown on the right, or plant it in a large container, as shown below. Stands 35" tall with container; 28" tall with just the stand.

Stand and 14" Basket Item #ZCK14
Stand and 16" Basket Item #ZCK16
Stand Alone Item #ZCKSA

Window Boxes

Window Box Planters WITH ATTACHED LINERS*
For use on Windows, Walls and Railings
They can also be used directly on Decks and Patios using Pot Toe supports.

Constructed from heavy gauge steel bars, coated in black plastic.
Flat bottoms make them easy to plant and transport.

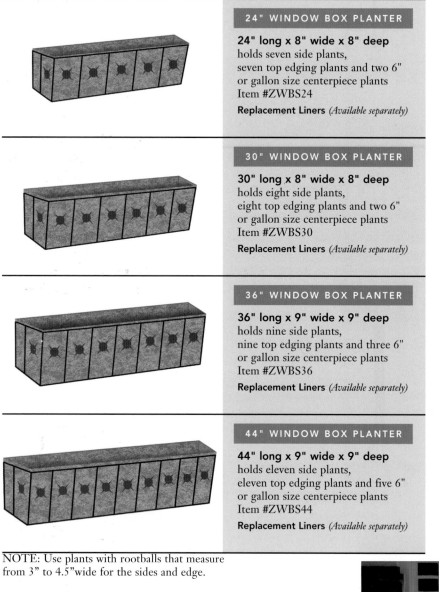

24" WINDOW BOX PLANTER

24" long x 8" wide x 8" deep
holds seven side plants,
seven top edging plants and two 6"
or gallon size centerpiece plants
Item #ZWBS24
Replacement Liners (*Available separately*)

30" WINDOW BOX PLANTER

30" long x 8" wide x 8" deep
holds eight side plants,
eight top edging plants and two 6"
or gallon size centerpiece plants
Item #ZWBS30
Replacement Liners (*Available separately*)

36" WINDOW BOX PLANTER

36" long x 9" wide x 9" deep
holds nine side plants,
nine top edging plants and three 6"
or gallon size centerpiece plants
Item #ZWBS36
Replacement Liners (*Available separately*)

44" WINDOW BOX PLANTER

44" long x 9" wide x 9" deep
holds eleven side plants,
eleven top edging plants and five 6"
or gallon size centerpiece plants
Item #ZWBS44
Replacement Liners (*Available separately*)

NOTE: Use plants with rootballs that measure
from 3" to 4.5"wide for the sides and edge.

J Hooks
For Window Boxes and Wall Planters

J Hooks are ideal for holding small to medium planters up to 36" on windows, walks and railings. For larger wall containers, use plated lag bolts or carriage bolts about 2.5" long with 1.5" o.d. washers. Masonry requires plastic anchors for masonry bolts and washers.

Item #KCJH (2 per pack)

Pot Toes
For Window Boxes (see photos below)

Prevents staining and rotting to decks and patios. Strong plastic tested to carry 500 lbs. To double their height, link them in pairs. On a slope, use Pot Toes on one side to level your pots.

Terracotta Pot Toes
Item #PT12TCHT (12 pot toes)
Black Pot Toes
Item #PT12BLHT (12 pot toes)

Left: Plastic pot toes

Right: Pot toes under a window box

* Patent pending

For product sources, see page 15.

Wall Planters WITH ATTACHED LINERS*
For use on Walls, Fences, Porch and Deck Railings
Constructed from heavy gauge steel wire coated in black plastic.

16" SINGLE WALL PLANTER

16" long x 8" wide x 7" deep
holds six side plants,
six top edging plants and one 6"
or gallon size centerpiece plant
Item #ZHBS16

Replacement Liners *(Available separately)*

20" SINGLE WALL PLANTER

20" long x 10" wide x 7" deep
holds eight side plants,
six top edging plants and two 6"
or gallon size centerpiece plants
Item #ZHBS20

Replacement Liners *(Available separately)*

20" DOUBLE WALL PLANTER

20" long x 10" wide x 10" deep
holds twelve side plants,
twelve top edging plants and two 6"
or gallon size centerpiece plants
Item #ZHBD20

Replacement Liners *(Available separately)*

NOTE: Use plants with rootballs that measure
from 3" to 4.5"wide for the sides and edge.

Where to Buy

From garden centers
Go to www.sideplanting.com to find a list of garden centers near you.
This is a great choice because you can pick up the plants and potting mix
at the same time.

Online
Go to www.kinsmangarden.com for retail and
www.kinsmanwholesale.com for wholesale.

Phone
1-800-733-4146 for retail orders or
1-800-733-5613 for wholesale orders.

Window Box or Wall Planter Brackets
For use on Decks with Wooden Railings
The top of each bracket has an
adjustable slide that moves to fit the
exact width of your railing, then it
fastens securely with a locking
screw. At the rear, the bracket
clamps around the underside of the
railing. The lower part of each
bracket goes down straight and
rigid, holding your planter away
from contact with the railings.

Each bracket is 13" tall. Adjusts
across top from 3.25" to 5.25"
wide. Grips lumber up to 1.75"
thick. For thinner lumber, shims
can be inserted to achieve a tight
fit.

Item #KCRB (2per pack)

* Patent pending

Choosing Basket Sizes...

Advantages of Baskets with One Side Layer (Single Baskets)

14" Single Side Layer Basket

❀ Single baskets weigh quite a bit less than the doubles. I can easily lift the two baskets shown on this page when they are full. I can't lift the two, larger doubles shown on the opposite page.

❀ Single baskets grow huge if you use great potting mix and fertilizer (see page 26).

❀ These smaller baskets require fewer plants than the larger ones.

16" Single Side Layer Basket

For product sources, see page 15.

They All Grew Bigger than I Anticipated!

Advantages of Baskets with Two Side Layers (Double Baskets)

❊ Double baskets require water less frequently than the smaller baskets do.

❊ Plants grow larger and live a bit longer in larger baskets.

Why do the plants in these containers grow so large?

❊ The plants don't grow anywhere near as large without the proper potting mix and fertilizer (see page 26).

❊ Horticulturists tell me the holes in the sides of the liners cause an oxygen increase in the potting mix, which encourages larger growth.

16" Double Side Layer Basket

20" Double Side Layer Basket

Materials: This basket requires 16 side and edge plants and 1 centerpiece. Five rust coleus, 6 creeping Jenny, and 5 red-and-yellow coleus will form the sides and edges. They are all planted in 4" pots. The grass (in a 1 gallon pot) is for the centerpiece.

Gather these together with potting mix, fertilizer (if not included in your potting mix), a bucket of water, a hose, and a small shovel.

Spray the container with water to soften the coco fiber.

Step 1: Add potting mix up to the bottom of the first hole. I prefer dry mix, while others prefer it wet. Using wet potting mix minimizes its loss through the holes while you are planting. Since this loss is minimal, I use the dry mix because it weighs less, making it easier to move the container after planting.

Step 2: Remove the first side plant from its pot. Just turn the pot upside down and pull the pot off.

Step 3: Dip the roots in water, and keep them submerged until they are completely saturated. If you see bubbles in the water, they are not yet saturated. Remove the plant, and squeeze the root ball 3 to 6 times - <u>very</u> firmly - until most of the water has dripped out.

Step 4: The root ball should be firm, not falling apart. If it still feels loose, squeeze it some more, until it is quite firm. (If some small pieces break off, that is ok - these are tough plants! I have had some root balls fall completely apart. I thought they would die, but planted them anyway, and they did just fine!)

Step 5: Push the root ball through the first hole, from the outside in. Don't worry if some potting mix falls off the root ball. That is normal.

Step 6: Be sure the plant is on the outside of the container and the roots are on the inside. Adjust the flap so it fits in between the roots and the plant.

Step 7: You will see some open space between the plant and the top of the hole. That is normal. Very little potting mix escapes from this opening because the roots grow together quickly, forming a solid mass.

Step 8: Alternate the three small plants around the sides.

(After I finish each layer, I wash off the table and the plants to remove any unwanted dirt. Be gentle with the plants!)

For product sources, see page 15.

Time: About 10 to 15 minutes!

Step 9: After planting the sides, remove the growing pot from the centerpiece, and put the plant in the middle of the new container. Measure with your fingers to see how much potting mix you need to bring the top of the centerpiece to about 1/2" above the top edge of container.

Step 10: Take the centerpiece out and add the necessary potting mix.

Step 11: Place the centerpiece in the middle of the pot, on top of the potting mix you just added. Add more potting mix around the centerpiece to bring the potting mix up to about 2" below the rim of the pot.

Step 12: After soaking the first edge plant in water and squeezing it, place it over a different plant – at an angle so it leans slightly over the edge. You don't need to squeeze the plant as much for the edge as you did for the sides. A larger root ball fits well here. Continue alternating plants until the edge is planted.

Step 13: Look between the root balls for any empty spots.

Step 14: Add potting mix between the root balls, as well as on any exposed roots, and pat it down slightly. Don't pile the potting mix up around the stems!

Wash the plants off very softly with the hose to remove any dirt from the leaves and stems.

Step 15: Fertilize with the product shown on page 26.

Step 16: Move your finished container to its chosen spot. Do not water it for at least 3 days because the roots are already soaked. After the first watering, add more potting mix with your fingers to fill in any spaces that appear between the plants.

Materials: This basket requires 30 side and edge plants and centerpiece plants. Ten purple petunias, 10 red and orange coleus and 10 wax begonias will form the sides and edges. The petunias and coleus are in 4" pots, while the begonias are in an 18-pack. Th 3 centerpiece plants, Persian shield, are in 1 gallon pots.

Gather these together with potting mix, fertilizer (if not included i your potting mix), a bucket of water, a hose, and a small shovel Scissors can also come in handy.

Step 1: Spray the container with water to soften the coco fiber.

Step 2: Add potting mix up to the bottom of the first hole. I prefer dry mix, while others prefer it wet. Using wet potting mix minimizes its loss through the holes while you are planting. Since this loss is minimal, I use the dry mix because it weighs less, making it easier to move the container after planting.

Step 3: Remove the first side plant from its pot. Just turn the pot upside down and pull the pot off.

Step 4: Dip the roots in water and keep them submerged unti they are completely saturated. I you see bubbles in the water they are not yet saturated Remove the plant and squeeze the root ball 3 to 6 times – very firmly – until most of the water has dripped out.

Step 5: The root ball should be firm, not falling apart. If it still feels loose, squeeze it some more, until it is quite firm. (If some small pieces break off, that is ok - these are tough plants! I have had some root balls fall completely apart. I thought they would die, but planted them anyway, and they did fine!)

Step 6: Push the root ball through the first hole, from the outside in. Don't worry if some potting mix falls off the root ball. That is normal.

Step 7: Be sure the plant is on the outside of the container and the roots are on the inside. Adjust the flap so it fits in between the roots and the plant.

Open space between plant and liner

Step 8: You will see some open space between the plant and the top of the hole. That is normal. Very little potting mix escapes from this opening because the roots grow together quickly, forming a solid mass.

For product sources, see page 15.

Step 9: Alternate the petunias and coleus around the bottom layer on the side. Fertilize* when you are done.

Wash the bottom layer of plants gently with water.

Step 10: Add potting mix up to the bottom of the next layer of holes.

Step 11: Plant the second layer in the same, alternating arrangement you used on the first layer. Be sure to plant different plants above each other. Fertilize when you are done.* Wash the plants gently to clean off the dirt.

Step 12: This photo shows the inside of the pot after planting the second layer. Patting the roots down slightly positions the plants upward on the outside of the container.

Step 13: Remove the growing pot from the centerpieces and put the plants in the middle of the new container. Measure with your fingers to see how much potting mix you need to add or remove to bring the top of the centerpiece to about 1/2" above the top edge. Adjust the level of the potting mix.

Step 14: To prepare to plant the edge layer, add potting mix around the centerpiece until it is about 2" below the rim of the container.

Step 15: After soaking the first edge plant in water and squeezing it, place it over a different type of plant. Angle it so it leans slightly over the edge. You don't need to squeeze the plant as much for the edge as you did for the sides. A larger root ball fits well here. Continue alternating plants until the edge is planted.

Step 16: Look between the root balls for any empty spots.

Step 17: Add potting mix between the root balls, as well as on any exposed roots and pat it down slightly. Don't pile the potting mix up around the stems!

Wash the plants off very softly with the hose to remove any dirt from the leaves and stems.

Step 18: Fertilize with the product shown on page 26.

Step 19: Move your finished container to its chosen spot. Do not water for at least 3 days because the roots are already soaked. After the first watering, add more potting mix with your fingers to fill in any spaces that appear between the plants.

**Many petunias did not like to be side planted. We had good luck with Wave petunias (Ball Seed) as well as Supertunias (Proven Winners).

Wall Pot Demo

Step 1: After hanging the basket (see page 25 for instructions), spray it with water to soften the coco fiber. Add potting mix up to the bottom of the first hole. Be sure to use top quality potting mix with a brand name you trust. Do not use garden soil or top soil because these soils are too heavy and can kill the plants.

Work with wet or dry potting mix. If it is wet, you will lose less through the holes during planting.

Step 2: Remove the first side plant from the pot. Dip the roots in a bucket of water, keeping them submerged until they are completely saturated. Remove the plant, and squeeze the root ball 3 to 6 times – <u>very</u> firmly – until most of the water has dripped out. (Plants with 4.5" root balls require more squeezing than plants with 3" root balls). The root ball should be firm, not falling apart. If it still feels loose, squeeze it some more, until it is quite firm.

(If some small pieces break off, that is ok - the plants we recommend are tough plants! I have had some root balls fall completely apart. I thought they would die, but planted them anyway, and they did just fine!)

Step 3: Push the root ball through the first hole, from the outside in. Don't worry if some potting mix falls off the root ball or out of the hole. That is normal. Be sure the plant is on the outside of the container and the roots are on the inside. Adjust the flap so it fits in between the roots and the plant.

You will see some open space between the plant and the top of the hole. That is normal. After the initial planting, very little potting mix escapes from this opening because the roots grow quickly, forming a solid mass.

Step 4: Alternate the small plants around the sides. Fertilize with the product sold on page 26. If your potting mix includes fertilizer, skip this step now, adding more only if the plants' leaves lose their color. The slow-release fertilizers usually last for the life of the basket.

Add the centerpiece plant, adjusting the height of the soil so the top of the root ball is about 1/2" above the top edge of the basket.

Step 5: Add more potting mix until it reaches the bottom of the second layer of side holes. Alternate the small plants in these openings. Plant different plants over each other.

Step 6: After soaking the first edge plant in water, squeeze it slightly between your hands to flatten it a bit – like a sandwich. Place it over a different plant, at an angle, so it leans slightly over the edge. Continue alternating plants until the edge is planted.

Add potting mix between the root balls, as well as on any exposed roots, and pat it down slightly. Don't pile the potting mix up around the stems! Fertilize again.

Do not water your finished container for about 3 days. Only water when the potting mix feels dry or the plants are wilted.

For product sources, see page 15.

Window Box Demo

Step 1: After hanging the box (see page 25 for instructions), spray it with water to soften the coco fiber. Add potting mix up to the bottom of the first hole. Be sure to use top quality potting mix with a brand name you trust. Do not use garden soil or top soil because these soils are too heavy and can kill the plants.

Work with wet or dry potting mix. If it is wet, you will lose less through the holes during planting.

Step 2: Remove the first side plant from the pot. Dip the roots in a bucket of water, keeping them submerged until they are completely saturated. Remove the plant, and squeeze the root ball 3 to 6 times - <u>very</u> firmly - until most of the water has dripped out. (Plants with 4.5" root balls require more squeezing than plants with 3" root balls). The root ball should be firm, not falling apart. If it still feels loose, squeeze it some more, until it is quite firm.

(If some small pieces break off, that is ok - the plants we recommend are tough plants! I have had some root balls fall completely apart. I thought they would die, but planted them anyway, and they did just fine!)

Step 3: Push the root ball through the first hole, from the outside in (root ball first). Don't worry if some potting mix falls off the root ball or out of the hole. That is normal. Be sure the plant is on the outside of the box and the roots are on the inside. Adjust the flap so it fits in between the roots and the plant.

You will see some open space between the plant and the top of the hole. That is normal, and some potting mix will escape during the planting process. However, after the initial planting, very little potting mix escapes from this opening because the roots grow quickly, forming a solid mass.

Step 4: Alternate the small plants around the sides. Fertilize with the product shown on page 26. If your potting mix includes fertilizer, skip this step now, adding more only if the plants' leaves lose their color. The slow release fertilizers usually last for the life of the basket.

Expect the side plants to droop a bit for the first few days. They grow up towards the sun after a little while.

Step 5: Add the centerpiece plants, adjusting the height of the soil underneath them so the top of the root ball is about 1/2" above the top edge of the basket.

Add more potting mix, up to about 1/2" from the top edge of the basket.

Step 6: After soaking the first edge plant in water, squeeze it slightly between your hands to flatten it a bit – like a sandwich. Place it in the basket, at an angle, so it leans slightly over the edge. Continue alternating plants until the edge is planted.

Add potting mix between the root balls, as well as on any exposed roots and pat it down slightly. Don't pile the potting mix up around the stems! Fertilize again.

Do not water your finished container for about 3 days. Only water when the potting mix feels dry or the plants are wilted.

Columns, Stands, Window Boxes

Assembling and Installing Border Columns

A Steel disk with gripping clips and central locator pin

B Square black wooden column

C 18" Steel ground spike

Tools needed:

Screwdriver, electric drill, sledge hammer, small level, flat piece of scrap wood (a 6" x 6" piece of a 2" x 6" board works fine; it's easy to find one at your local home improvement store.)

Check to be sure you have all the components:

A. Steel disk assembly for top of column

B. Black wooden column

C. Steel ground spike

D. Bag of hardware (not shown)

To assemble and install:

1. Put the piece of scrap wood on top of the square column so the sledge hammer doesn't damage the metal column. Drive the ground spike into the earth with a sledge hammer until only the square column holder is above the surface. Check to be sure it is level after each few hits with the hammer both vertically and horizontally. This keeps the column from being crooked.

2. Place the wooden column into the top of the ground spike.

3. Drill starter holes into the column through the holes in the ground spike.

4. Insert wood screws and tighten.

6. Place steel disk assembly on top of the column.

7. Insert wood screws, and tighten.

Assembling Patio Stands

Both patio stands are very easy to put together with just a few screws.

Instructions are included. Putting together the smaller stand (shown right) is shown on the video clip at www.sideplanting.com. It only takes about thirty seconds!

For product sources, see page 15.

Placing the Basket on Top of the Column

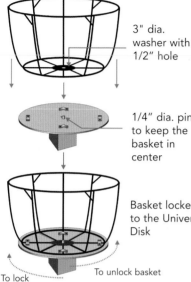

3" dia. washer with 1/2" hole

1/4" dia. pin to keep the basket in center

Basket locked to the Universal Disk

To lock basket in position

To unlock basket

1. Place any of the four Basic Basket Planters onto the disk, so the center locator pin fits into center hole of basket bottom.

2. The baskets can be empty or filled with plants. That is your choice.

3. Rotate basket clockwise until disk grips wires.

4. Very important! It is easy to see if the four holders on the disk are firmly attached to the wires if the basket is empty (minus the liner) because you can see the attachments. Not so if it is full. If this is the case, look in between the basket and the metal assembly. If you see light, at least one of the holders is not attached. Remove it, and repeat. If the basket is not firmly attached to all four holders, it will fall off! This happened to me, and my lovely basket toppled over in the first breeze. I will never make that mistake again!

4. You can turn the basket every week or so to achieve even growth. Just rotate counter-clockwise until the back is at the front; then, turn clockwise to lock again. Or you can lift off the basket and replace it with another freshly planted basket at any time.

Installing Window Boxes and Wall Planters

Hardware to use:

Fasteners for the window boxes and wall planters are not included in the box since different uses require different types of fasteners.

Wood siding and railings: Hold empty container in place, and drill pilot holes at the bumps in the top rear bar. Then install J-hooks (shown left). If you prefer to use screws to hold up your container, place one every 12 inches. Wall planters hold well with simple screws at the bumps, but some people prefer the look of J-hooks. See page 14 for buying information.

Masonry: Same as wood siding, but make holes in masonry (with a masonry drill bit) large enough to install plastic anchors for J-hooks. Alternatively, bolts with washers may be used to grip the 'bumps' in the containers.

Alternative for railings for window boxes: Brackets (shown below) can be used to hold any size window box. See page 15 for more information on the brackets.

Potting Mix & Fertilizer

Potting Mix

Don't skimp on your potting mix. Good potting mix costs a little bit more, but makes all the difference. The plants grow larger and live longer with quality potting mix. Do not buy topsoil for containers. It is too heavy, and the plants may rot and die quickly.

Look for a brand name you trust. Peters, Miracle Grow, Lambert's and Fafard (along with many others) offer top-quality potting soil.

Look for a potting mix with fertilizer and/or water saving polymers mixed in. This will save you some time.

New Fertilizer is a No Brainer: Just Apply Once

Fertilizer is one of the most important components of easy container gardens. Without the right fertilizer, plants will slowly turn yellow and decline.

I have only found one fertilizer that works perfectly every time. And it is forgiving. If you use too much, it doesn't burn the plants. It also is excellent for the environment, winning the 2005 Gulf Guardian Award from the EPA Gulf of Mexico Program Partnership.

This fertilizer is slow-release, meaning its little pellets release the nutrients over a period of time. It is a great improvement over the liquids you apply weekly with a hose sprayer! However, there are many slow-release products on the market. I have tested every one I could get my hands on, and none come close to this one. Some either don't last as long or don't have all the nutrients plants need. Others release all their nutrients at once if there is a lot of rain, burning the plants.

This fertilizer lasts nine months in 'average' conditions. If you see the plants yellowing a bit, just add some more. Sprinkle it on top of the potting mix, following the instructions on the label.

Many potting mixes also include fertilizer. I haven't found one yet that lasts long, so I add this one at planting time as well. **This fertilizer is available at www.kinsmangarden.com.**

Look for These Ingredients on the Label

I have killed many plants with the wrong fertilizer. I have also been through fertilizers that simply didn't make the grade. They included some but not all of the elements a plant needs. Weird, hard-to-diagnose nutritional deficiencies developed that were time consuming, annoying, and definitely not easy.

Plants are like people - they need lots of different nutrients to keep them alive. If you have a vitamin deficiency, you might get quite sick. Same thing for a plant. Learn to read the fertilizer label to make sure it includes *all* the nutrients your plants need.

Most fertilizers include nitrogen, phosphorus (phosphate), and potassium (potash). Most, including some of the best-selling brands, don't include the micronutrients that plants need. **So look for boron, copper, iron, manganese, and magnesium as well. Do not buy a product that doesn't include these micronutrients, or your plants could suffer later.**

For product sources, see page 15.

Pinching, Trimming, & Replacing Plants

Pinching and Trimming

If plants look leggy or uneven, pinch or trim off the unwanted portions. Use your finger or pruning shears (if the stem is too thick). See the plant profiles for individual pinching and cut-back requirements. The plant in the first photo has a bulge on the right side near the top. It is easy to pinch the plants to even it out.

Replacing Plants

About one per cent of the plants we used in instant containers died in our trials. Replacing them is easy, as shown below. It can be difficult, however, to find the same plant at your garden center. I used whatever I could find that was similar. For example, the torenia that needed replacing below was purple. The closest I could find was blue, which worked out just fine.

1. Pull the plant you want to replace out by its roots. Get as much of the roots as you can, without disturbing its neighbors.

2. Try to reduce the roots of the new plant (dip them in water first) to match the size of the one you took out. If the new one is a bit larger, it's ok.

3. Use a spoon to hollow out space for the new plant. The hole can be smaller than the roots because they compress when you plant them.

4. Insert the roots into the hole.

5. Press it in as best you can, so it doesn't fall out. It will root in quickly.

6. Although the new plant is smaller than its neighbors, it fills in quickly.

Watering...

General

Watering takes the most time of any container garden chore. Plants in containers need more water than plants in the ground because their root systems are smaller, and the roots are where plants store most of their water. The root system of a plant in the ground is three times the diameter of the plant. Not so for container plants - the roots are only as large as the container.

I was pleasantly surprised by the watering needs of instant containers. Prior to using them, I was concerned that the coco fiber would not hold water for long. I pictured myself permanently standing next to a container pouring water on it! Luckily, that was not the case. Read these two pages to learn what it took me hundreds of trials to master.

Factors That Affect Water Use

✽ **Sun or shade.** Plants use a third to half as much water in shade than in full sun.

✽ **Temperature.** Plants use more water when the temperatures are high.

✽ **Wind.** Plants in windy areas require more water than plants in calm areas.

✽ **Reflections from walls.** If you have a light-colored wall facing south with no shade, you may have to plant - succulents to take the reflected heat if you live in a very hot climate.

✽ **Soil.** Good-quality potting mix usually includes peat moss, which holds water better than cheaper, sandy soils.

✽ **Plant type.** Plant species vary in their need for water. Impatiens, for example, need much more water than cactus.

✽ **Container size.** Large containers with small plants require much less water than small containers filled to the brim with large plants.

✽ **How long the plant has been in the container.** As plants age in containers, their roots fill the pot, leaving less space for water.

How to Tell When a Plant Needs Water

Water when you see signs of wilt or the soil feels dry to the touch. Use your finger to test the soil. Push it into the soil about an inch or so. Low-water plants like cacti and succulents, need less water and can go longer with dry soil.

Knowing when to water is very important because many container plants die from overwatering. If the plant looks wilted and the soil has been wet for several days, the plant has drowned and will probably die. It has a fungus. You might try a fungicide if the plant is very important to you.

How Much Water to Apply

Water thoroughly with each application. The biggest watering mistake people make is to give the plant just a little bit of water. That is the same as giving a person dying of thirst just a teaspoonful of water! Soak the plant thoroughly until you see a steady stream of water coming out of the bottom of the pot. A slow soaking is better than a fast hit with the hose because it allows the roots time to absorb the water.

For product sources, see page 15.

Watering Details: Drip Irrigation is the Easiest

Above: Be sure to water the basket thoroughly and evenly, until the water comes out of the bottom. This wand that fits on the end of a hose is great for watering baskets.

Above: Our baskets on columns get water from the sprinklers that water the garden. We supplement with hand watering as needed because the baskets sometimes need more water than the landscape plantings.

The most common reason for plant death in hanging baskets is overwatering. The plants placed through the sides of the basket retain water longer than the plants placed on the top. When we first planted these baskets, we had them in a section of the nursery that gets daily water. After a few weeks of this drenching, many of the plants placed on the sides of the baskets died. When I checked them with my finger, the soil around them was completely soaked, and I realized I had drowned the poor things. We replaced the dead plants and moved the baskets to another area where we could water less frequently. I began to check the soil under the coco fiber at the base of the side plantings before watering. We had no more unexpected plant fatalities.

The baskets we planted in March in Florida on average needed water every three days when they were placed in light shade*. As the plants grew and the days warmed, we increased the water to every other day. In the heat of summer, when the plants are fully grown, plan on daily watering if the plants are in the sun. Some of the thirstiest plants, like sweet potato vines, need water twice a day in full sun in the summer. If the temperatures are in the mid-90's or above and the baskets are in full sun, they might need water twice a day.

Baskets in very windy locations are hard to manage. The wind dries them out quickly, so be prepared to water often before making the decision to use them in a windy spot.

If your plant shows signs of wilt, water it. Otherwise, use your finger to see if the soil is dry before watering.

We used three different systems for watering our baskets: hand watering, drip irrigation, and in-ground sprinklers (the same ones that water the garden). Hand watering is the most time consuming. The drip system worked pretty well. My friend, Tim Hadsell, installed it, and it didn't take too long. He ran a black flexible pipe from my hose bib to the pots. Tiny black tubes (I call them spaghetti tubes) ran from the larger pipe to the pots. Little emitters were attached to the tubes and stuck into the pot. Different kinds of emitters fit different pots. We hooked it to a timer, which I found difficult to use, so I just turned on the hose when I wanted to water, and all the pots connected to the drip system got watered at the same time.

I found a few disadvantages to the drip system. Be sure the piece that attaches to your hose has a filter so that the emitters don't get clogged. Well water clogs them up more than city water. Also, sometimes an emitter would fall out of a pot, and I would not notice it until the plant wilted. Another disadvantage is that all the plants on the same system get watered at the same time. Some may need it when others don't. **However, after going through a summer when the temperatures went over 100 degrees for 10 days straight, I will always have drip systems in my pots in the future.**

Our baskets on columns get water from our in-ground sprinkler system most of the time. We water our gardens twice a week if it isn't raining. When the weather is hot and the basket is big, twice a week is not enough, so we supplement with hand watering.

*See details of watering differences in diverse trial areas on page 7.

Chapter 2

Container Design

16" basic basket

Edge Plants   **Centerpieces**   **Side Plants**

30" window box

Centerpiece

Edge Plants

Side Plants

Whether you know it or not, you are a born designer. There is special place in your brain that tells you what shirt to wear with that blue pair of pants, what throw pillow to choose for your couch. This subtle part of your brain doesn't scream the answers to you - it whispers them.

Let's call it your design instinct. Listen to it, because it guides you to make the right choices. Use this instinct, coupled with these instructions, to design your personal masterpieces.

❀ Choose your centerpiece
   - Tips for choosing a great centerpiece
   - 10 best centerpiece plants

❀ Choose your side and edge plants
   - Which plants do best
   - 10 best side and edge plants

❀ Choose your planting pattern

Plus...
   - Tips for professional results
   - Assessing your light levels

Left: This basket has one plant for the centerpiece, a caladium. The edge plants (New Guinea impatiens) are different from the side plants (begonias and polka dot plants).

Above: This window box has two different kinds of plants for the centerpiece - Bok choy and dwarf striped sweet flag grass. The side and edge plants are mixed pansies.

Step 1: Choose a Centerpiece...

A centerpiece is a plant that is planted in the middle of an arrangement. I usually choose the centerpiece first and like to do this at the garden center. It becomes the focal point of the arrangement. I carry it around on a shopping cart to see which other plants I like with it.

Choose a Centerpiece that Stays Taller than the Surrounding Plants, even When They are Mature.

Centerpiece plants should remain taller than the surrounding plants for the life of the arrangement. The *Carex* grass (shown at left) is an example of a good choice because it will always be taller than the surrounding coleus.

The dwarf striped sweet flag grass (right) is perfectly sized for the surrounding pansies. They will never outgrow the grass. However, look at the same grass in the photo (below, left). The coleus and begonias grew taller than the grass.

Common Mistake: Planting a Centerpiece that is too Short

Before

After

The window box shown (left and right) is the same box moved from a deck railing to a different location under a window. The centerpiece was changed because the coleus and begonias grew taller than the dwarf striped sweet flag grass, shown left. The *Juncus* grass, shown right, is taller and a much better choice for this arrangement.

Use Full Centerpieces

Several salvia plants, grouped together, form a full centerpiece.

This single delphinium is too skinny for this arrangement.

I planted three salvias - two red and one purple – in the center of the 14" basket shown left. One plant would have looked too skinny.

The blue delphiniums in the basket shown right are too skinny for the overall size of the arrangement. I should have massed more of them together for a full look.

For product sources, see page 15.

Tips for the Best Choice

Use a Centerpiece that is a Different Texture from the Surrounding Plants.

One of the easiest plans for container gardens is to use a spiky centerpiece – like the dracaena, shown left – surrounded by mounded and/or trailing plants. I don't do this with every container I plant, but it is a great tool for instant success. Grasses, ti plants, and dracaenas are all good choices for spiky centerpieces.

Large-leafed plants, like caladiums (right), are also great for varying texture.

Single Centerpieces

When only one type of plant is used in the center of an arrangement, it's called a single centerpiece. I suggest this for beginners because it is easy!

The basket shown left has just one centerpiece, a lime green coleus.

The basket shown right also has just one centerpiece, a grass.

Double Centerpieces

When two different types of plants are used in an arrangement, it's called a double centerpiece. This is a good technique for experienced container gardeners.

Both baskets shown here have pentas and blue salvia as their centerpieces. This worked fairly well, but would have worked better had I put the salvia in the center and the pentas around it. When I bought the plants, the pentas were taller than the salvia, which led me to put them in the middle. But, the mature size of the salvia is taller than the pentas, so always know the mature size of the plants you use.

Top Ten Centerpieces...

Blue Salvia

Blue salvia is the ideal centerpiece because it is easy to maintain at a taller height than most side and edge plants. It also has a spiky texture that contrasts well with many small-leafed or round-flowered plants. And it's easy, blooms for months on end, and requires little care. (Plant profile, page 150)

Caladiums

Caladiums are ideal centerpieces. But like pentas, many sizes are on the market, and some of the dwarfs are too short. Most of the caladiums commonly sold at garden centers are the taller types, which are the choice for centerpieces. (Plant profile, page 139)

Dracaenas

Dracaenas work beautifully. I tried green, tricolor, and the newer lemon-lime (pictured) with great success. They have the perfect, spiky texture for centerpieces and are easy. No one kills dracaenas! (Plant profile, page 141)

Giant Coleus

Giant coleus (the Kong series) thrived as a centerpiece. Its large-leaf texture contrasted well with smaller-leafed plants. I used this coleus in the sides of baskets as well, where it stayed smaller than if it was planted in the top. (Plant profile, page 140)

Golden Shrimp

Golden shrimp plant (*Pachystachus lutea*) makes a great centerpiece. Be sure you get this specific type because many of the other shrimp plants are not upright growers. It blooms all season in light to medium shade and is very easy to grow. (Plant profile, page 151)

For product sources, see page 15.

Easy, Attractive, Long-lived

Grasses

Grasses are my favorite centerpiece plant. I've tried *Juncus spp.*, *Pennisetum spp.*, *Acorus spp.*, *Liriope spp.* (pictured), *Carex spp.*, and many others. Since the heights of grasses vary considerably, be sure your choice stays taller than the surrounding plants. (Plant profiles, pages 142, 145, 154, and 155)

Mona Lavender

Mona Lavender offers spiky texture, lots of flowers, and a full form. It blooms for four to six months in cool weather. It doesn't bloom in hot weather, however, so avoid it in Houston in August! (Plant profile, page 146)

Pentas

Pentas won the prize for attracting the most butterflies and bumble bees, but be sure you plant tall ones for centerpieces. Many sizes are on the market, and some of the dwarfs are too short. Pentas take heat well and bloom constantly. (Plant profile, page 149)

Persian Shield

Persian shield's chunky form and gorgeous leaves look wonderful as a centerpiece plant. It is easy to grow and thrives in sun or shade. (Plant profile, page 149)

Ti Plants

Ti plants are fabulous! Many types are available. Be sure to use several plants in each container if they are on the skinny side. All ti plants do quite well in light to medium shade. Some types do well in sun, also. (Plant profile, page 151)

Step 2: Choose Side & Edge Plants.

Once you have chosen your centerpiece, look for smaller plants with root-balls of 3" to 4.5" to plant in the sides and along the top edge. Use your instincts! See which combinations make you smile!

Limit the Number of Different Plants in the Beginning.

It is easiest to begin with only a few different kinds of plants. Use two or three different plants for the edges and the sides and simply alternate them. Use one more different plant for the centerpiece.

This simple choice makes shopping really easy – just pick a few plants that you like to see together.

The 14" basket (shown left) features a simple combination of a coleus as the centerpiece, with the sides and edges planted with another coleus and wax begonia, in an alternating pattern. What could be simpler?

Stick to Mounding Plants in the Beginning.

Mounding plants grow into compact, mound-like shapes. Trailing plants trail down like vines. Although trailing plants are quite attractive in instant containers, they are a bit trickier to use. So, stick to mounding plants in the beginning.

This 16" wall basket uses mounding impatiens and coleus in the sides and along the top edge. These are both really easy container plants, provided you place the impatiens in shade if it is hot.

Learn the Simple Trick of Alternating a Few Different Plants.

This container has only three kinds of coleus alternated in the sides and along the top edge. By alternating, the basket remains balanced. If you use too many different plants around the sides, your basket will not grow evenly. Or, if you plant one kind of plant on one side and another on the opposite side, the same unbalanced look will result.

Many of the baskets shown in this book were planted by inexperienced people who understood the alternating concept immediately!

The alternating method also makes figuring out the quantities of plants really easy. Simply divide the total number of plants needed by the number of different plants you choose. For example, if you choose three different plants for a 16" basket - which requires 24 side and edge plants – you'll need 8 of each.

For product sources, see page 15.

Tips for the Best Choices

Size Options for Side Plants: 3" Multipacks or Larger

Flats or multipacks

4.5" pots

Leggy plant from a flat

Above: If you plant leggy plants from flats, pinch them back so they will fill out. The basket may not look full on day one, but it will look better in the long run.

Baskets with side plantings require a lot of plants. We recommend either flats that hold multiple plants (with root balls of at least 3") or the individual plants in 4" or 4.5" pots. The size is an important consideration, because the plants in the multipacks cost considerably less.

Plants in multipacks are smaller than the plants in separate, 4" or 4.5" pots. Different garden centers sell different quantities in a flat, from 6 to 18. The 18-packs are commonly called '1801 packs.'

Advantages of mulitpacks compared with individual pots
❀ Less expensive
❀ Easier to transport

Disadvantages of flats compared with 4.5" pots:
❀ Plants in flats are harder to remove from the container. Don't pull the plant out from the top or you will tear the roots. Some flats have serrated sections so that you can pull individual cells apart. If yours doesn't, cut the container apart with scissors. Turn the individual cell upside down and squeeze the sides a bit so the root ball comes out easily.

❀ You'll need to plant the plants from flats within a few days of bringing them home because the plants are so close together that they will get leggy quickly (see photo, left). Or, you can cut or pull the individual cells apart and store them with space in between so they have room to spread. Plants in 4.5" pots can be kept for up to a month after buying them, depending on how root-bound they are.

❀ The plants in multipacks are smaller than the plants in individual, 4 or 4.5" containers. It takes longer for your container to fill in. If you plant an instant container from full, 4.5" pots, it usually looks very full on planting day. Planting from multipacks delays that fullness. However, the delay is quite short. Containers planted with plants from multipacks normally fill out in a week or two.

Planting Seedlings in Instant Containers

Above: Small seedlings require months to fill in. Use larger plants instead.

Instant containers were designed for instant impact. This impact is achieved by planting mature plants in them. However, I planted every size plant imaginable during our trials. Frequently, I would need a plant that wasn't locally available in mature sizes. Seedlings could be flown in from other locations, which greatly increased the numbers of different plants I could test.

Nurseries take seedlings and plant them into multipacks or individual pots, letting them grow for a few months so you can have large plants. I often didn't have time to do that, and simply planted the seedlings directly in the instant containers. I would put in as many as a hole would hold – generally three.

It would take at least a month for these containers to fill out. Had I only put one seedling in a hole, it could have taken up to three months, so I don't recommend it.

Begonias, Wax

Wax begonias are the number one plant for instant containers. They are not only easy to find and grow but also bloom continually. Look for the newer 'Gumdrops' begonia (shown right) which features a double flower. The pink color lit up our instant containers. (Plant profile, page 140)

Begonias, Dragon Wing

Dragon wing begonias were one of the best performers of our trials. They are slower to start than wax begonias but have a higher percentage of color in the long run. They also grow larger than wax begonias – large enough to crowd out their neighbors a bit. (Plant profile, page 138)

Coleus

Coleus is my favorite container plant. Its colors and patterns are endless. It usually requires some pinching to keep it from getting leggy, but that small task is well worth the trouble. I use it both as a centerpiece and as a side or edge plant. (Plant profile, page 140)

Creeping Jenny

I use creeping Jenny as a mounding or trailing plant. Its small leaves and lime-green color contrast well with most other plants. In most of the country, it is a perennial, so you can plant it in your garden after it finishes its time in the basket. (Plant profile, page 144)

Impatiens

Impatiens thrive in any location of the instant containers. We had great luck with regular impatiens (left) as well as double impatiens and 'Little Lizzie' impatiens. The red flowers in the container (shown right) are double impatiens, while the purples are 'Little Lizzie.' (Plant profiles, pages 144 and 154)

For product sources, see page 15.

Easy, Attractive, Long-lived

Ivy

Ivy is very useful in instant containers, especially because it is one of the few popular container plants that grows in deep shade. Since the side plants don't get as much light as the top plants, it is a good choice when used as shown (right). (Plant profile, page 144)

Lamium

Lamium is a trailing plant that is gaining favor in container gardens. I particularly like it with light colors, like purples and pinks. Although it is lovely in flower, its flowering season is short. Use this plant for its leaf color. (Plant profile, page 145)

Mint, Variegated

Variegated mint is not only easy to grow but also versatile. It grows with a mounding habit if trimmed, or a trailing habit if allowed to grow. The variegated leaves break up masses of green. (Plant profile, page 147)

Torenia, Trailing

Trailing torenia is a fabulous plant. It thrives for a long growing season, blooms in cool or very hot weather, and takes almost no care! It outperformed the upright torenia because it lived longer and didn't require any pinching back. (Plant profile, page 152)

Scaevola

Scaevola ('Blue Wonder', 'Whirlwind Blue' and 'Whirlwind White') performed very well in our trials. Unfortunately, an unexpected freeze killed the baskets with scaevola I was going to photograph for this book! They were gorgeous! (Plant profile, page 154)

Mixed Performers for the Sides

Upright Torenia

Petunia

Verbena

Sweet Potato Vines (all)

Lobelia

Periwinkle

The plants shown (left) rate mixed reviews.

The upright torenia, although I used it frequently and will continue to do so, did not live as long as the trailing type. It also drooped awkwardly after a while, requiring a cut-back that took a few weeks for recovery.

Trailing verbena did very well sometimes but stopped blooming in others. All of the upright verbena quickly died.

Petunias were the most confusing flower we tried – some of them thrived while others quickly died. We had the best luck with Easy Wave petunias. Proven Winners' Supertunias did very well, but a few of them died (after 18 inches of rain from a hurricane!)

Sweet potato vines did too well, taking over many of my baskets. I still use them, though, but carefully!

Lobelia worked sometimes and died other times. I love this plant, and will continue to try to succeed with it.

Periwinkles lived in Georgia, but not in Florida – probably because the rainfall is double in Florida. But their form wasn't ideal – they stuck out awkwardly.

Plants that Died Quickly in the Sides

Fuchsia

Snapdragon

Marigolds

Marguerite Daisy

Dusty Miller

Alyssum

The plants shown (left) died quickly in the sides of our baskets. However, most did quite well when planted in the top of the baskets, either as a centerpiece or as an edge plant.

Alyssum, for example, died in the sides but did quite well as an edge plant. See it (right) in a beautiful basket.

We don't know why these plants died, and it is possible that other cultivars of these same flowers could do well. We will keep testing, and you do the same. If you would like to share any of your experiences, contact us at info@sideplanting.com

Above: Although alyssum doesn't like being planted in the sides of a basket, it thrives on the top edge.
Below: Marguerite daisies thrive as a centerpiece.

For product sources, see page 15.

Working with Shade...

The Shade Test

Learn to understand your shade! To determine the degree of shade in your garden, try the following tests. Sit in the same location you are considering for a container and look around.

Mixed light: These areas get both direct sun and full shade and are normally found near buildings. The change in light is due to the movement of the sun, either from morning to evening or from winter to summer. If the movement is from winter to summer, it can be difficult to assess without a compass. Be sure to picture the seasonal sun movement when assessing the light. Plants in mixed light need the ability to adapt to extremes.

Some good choices for mixed light: Creeping Jenny, torenia, coleus, dwarf white striped sweet flag grass, and some begonias.

Light shade: Look up, and you will see about 20-30% leaves and the rest sky. The trees are planted farther apart in light shade than in medium shade. Look down, and notice many types of plants growing. Look around, and see many patches of sky from any direction.

Some good choices for light shade: begonias, bromeliads, caladiums, coleus, California daisy, creeping Jenny, geraniums, grasses, impatiens, ivy, lamium, *Lysimachia* 'Outback Sunset,' melampodium, Mona lavender, ornamental kale or cabbage, pansies, pentas, perilla, Persian shield, petunias, variegated mint, salvia, shrimp plants, sweet potatoes, ti plants, and violas.

Medium shade: Look up, and you will see medium shade from trees. Look for about 50% or more of sky. Look down and see ferns or other shade plants growing. Look around, and see more trees, but not much open sky on the south or west sides. Sun from the south or west is strong and too much for most medium shade plants.

Some good choices for medium shade: begonias, bromeliads, caladiums, dracaenas, impatiens, ivy, Persian shield, shrimp plants, ti plants, and violas.

Dense shade: Look up and you will see the dense shade of very thick trees, or the roof of a building. Less than 30% of the sky is visible. Look down and see almost nothing growing, except possibly a few weeds. Look all around, and you will still see very little sky, but rather more thickly-leafed trees or buildings.

Some good choices for dense shade: Anthuriums, bromeliads, dracaenas, ivy, peace lilies, and pothos. Check out the house plant section of your garden center for more choices.

For product sources, see page 15.

What to Plant?

Assessing Shade

As I design gardens, the most difficult challenge I face is assessing the degree of shade in any given spot. If the sun stayed in the same place all the time, it would be easy. But, it moves from east to west every day and from north to south every year.

I have developed a simple method, which works most of the time. Get a compass, and go to the spot you are considering. Pretend you are the container. Put your eye at the level of the plant and look around. Look up, down, and 360 degrees around. Since the sun moves throughout the day, do this mid-morning, noon, and mid-afternoon. This observation will give you a good understanding of the amount of light the container will receive at different times of the day.

Understand that the angle of the sun moves. At noon in June, the sun is almost straight overhead. At noon in December, it is further south. Imagine this change as you observe the sun. The seasonal difference can be significant for plants. Some locations are in full sun in summer and in medium shade during winter. I put sun plants in a container one summer, and they did well. The next winter, I planted pansies (in Georgia, where pansies thrive in winter) in the same location. They struggled, until I realized that the same spot was shady that time of year. Luckily, because the plants were in a container, I could move the whole thing to a sunny spot.

Above: Impatiens are one of the best plants for light to medium shade. They take sun if the days are short and the weather cool, like south Florida in the winter.

What to Plant in Dense Shade

Many plants thrive in light to medium shade. Dense shade, however, is a difficult situation. Most flowering plants require more light than dense shade provides. Stick to plants you find in the house plant section of your garden center for dense shade situations. Examples are shown to the right and left.

Rotating your Containers

If the front and back of your container gets completely different light conditions, you need to rotate it every few days. For a small hanging basket (14" or 16" single layer), use a swivlit basket ring (right) so that it is easy to rotate. See page 12 for more information.

If your basket is on a column, simply lift it off its base and rotate it 90 degrees. Be sure you re-attach it carefully when you are done, so it doesn't fall off its column. See page 25 for full instructions.

Above: Baskets hung on porches need to be rotated so that each side gets the same amount of light.

Step 3: Choose the Planting Plan...

There are thousands of different ways to arrange plants in these containers. Here are three of the easiest, which are also my favorites!

1-2-3 Planting Plans (Detailed in pages 46-81, 86-87, and 92-95)

Simple! Just alternate plants around the sides and edge, using a different centerpiece. This plan (left) alternates red begonias, 'Dark Star' coleus, and *Lysimachia* 'Outback Sunset.'

One of the biggest benefits of alternating plants is evenness. The basket grows uniformly, without bulges or thin spots.

❀ Use two, three, or four different plants.

❀ It's easiest to use all mounding plants.

❀ Put different plants above each other.

Layered Planting Plans (Detailed in Chapter 5, pages 100-115)

Layered plans have different plants on different layers. In other words, plant the sides in one pattern and the edge in another.

Layered plans have a manicured, organized look.

❀ This layered plan simply alternates two different colors of impatiens in the side holes.

❀ White begonias are planted around the edge.

Striped Planting Plans (Detailed on page 84-85)

Striped plans are similar to 1-2-3 plans in that they feature alternated plants around the side and edge layers. Also, the same plants are used on both layers.

The difference is that you place the same plant above itself. In other words, if you plant a coleus in the side hole, put another one above it on the edge layer.

Striped plans are used for long, trailing plants - keeping a long trailer from covering up a small, mounding plant that might be below it.

Striped plans work best in containers with only one layer of side holes.

For product sources, see page 15.

Plus Tips for Professional Results

Choose Companion Plants that Like the Same Growing Conditions.

If you are planting a basket for sun, be sure that all the plants you choose like sunny conditions.

The same goes for shade. Refer to the last chapter of this book to learn the light conditions of each plant.

The basket shown left is in light shade, which is the easiest light condition for containers. It includes double impatiens, sweet potato vines, 'Supertunias' (petunias), and snapdragons.

Choose Different Sizes and Shapes of Flowers.

Look at the difference in size of the flowers in the basket shown to the left. The red verbena are large and the blue lobelia is small. That size difference helps the eye differentiate between the different plants and is quite appealing.

Different flower textures work well, too. Look at the difference between the spiky salvia and the round pentas shown to the right. This combination is easy to find and easy to grow!

Leftover Baskets

These baskets follow no plan whatsoever.

We started making them when we had odd numbers of plants leftover from other wonderfully organized baskets.

This is a good idea for the non-conformist, the person who does not like rules or patterns. And it's a lot of fun to boot!

Chapter 3

1-2-3 Designs
with Mounding Plants

20" double wall basket

2 Centerpieces

Different
Plants are
Placed on Top
of Each Other

4 Side and Edge Plants, Alternated

Ti Plant
(1 plant from a 3-gallon pot)
Plant Profile: Page 146

Canna Lily
(2 plants from 1-gallon pots)

Coleus 'Wizard Rose'
(5 plants from 4.5" pots)
Plant Profile: Page 134

Upright Torenia
(5 plants from 4.5" pots)
Plant Profile: Page 147

Dragon Wing Begonia
(5 plants from 4.5" pots)
Plant Profile: Page 132

Coleus 'Bellingrath'
(5 plants from 4.5" pots)
Plant Profile: Page 134

Characteristics of 1-2-3 designs:

❀ Alternate between two and four different plants around both the sides and the edge.

❀ Place different plants above one another for a mosaic look.

❀ Plant a contrasting centerpiece.

Benefits of 1-2-3 designs with mounding plants:

❀ Even growth habit

❀ Easy to design and plant

❀ Easy to figure out how many plants you need - just look at the number needed for the sides and edge and divide by the number of different plants (see pages 12, 14, and 15 for the number needed for each of the different containers). For example, the 20" double wall basket (shown) requires 20 side and edge plants. Since this one features four different plants around the sides and edge, divide 20 by four, which is five.

Left: This container is one of the early prototypes I planted. It is actually larger than the 20" double wall planter (shown opposite). But the combination would work best in that size, rather than the larger one shown here. The plant quantities (shown) work in the 20" double wall basket.

The only mistake I made was planting canna lilies in the top. The label said 'dwarf canna,' and I thought it would top out at about 2' tall. Not so. It rocketed up to over 4' tall, and we had to cut it down because it ruined the proportion of the arrangement. So much for 'dwarf' plants! Luckily, the pot had so many plants in it that the cannas were not even missed.

Simple Wall Basket

16"single wall basket

Salvia, coleus, and begonias team up to create an easy arrangement - both to plant and to maintain. The salvia forms the centerpiece, and the other three plants are simply alternated around the edge and side. These tried-and-true plants have been high performers for generations. The color contrast of dark purple and lime green gives this small arrangement its punch.

Planting Sequence

Step 1: For the side layer, alternate the begonias with the two colors of coleus.

Step 2: Plant the two salvias close together in the center.

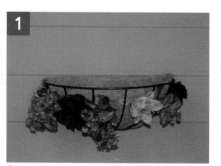

Step 3: Repeat Step 1 around the edge. Be sure to put different plants above each other. *(For full planting demo, see page 22.)*

Cultural Information

Light: Full sun to light shade. Since wax begonias are sold for sun or shade, be sure to choose those that fit your light situation. Most take sun until the temperatures hit the low 90's. The red-leafed varieties take sun in higher temperatures, along with some of the newer, green-leafed types that should be labeled as sun begonias.

Season: Spring through fall for most areas. Also thrives in winter in areas where the temperatures stay above 38 degrees. This plant mix takes temperatures from about 38 degrees to the low 90's in full sun. In light shade, it withstands higher temperatures into the high 90's.

Lifespan: Two to four months in this container. Plants in small wall baskets live shorter lives than those planted in larger containers.

Care: Fertilize on planting day with the slow-release mix described on page 26. Repeat if the leaves look yellowish or washed-out, although the fertilizer should last from six to nine months. Remove the dead flowers from the salvia if you feel energetic!

Water: Water when the plants show signs of wilt or the soil feels dry when you push your fingertip up to your second knuckle into the potting mix. I watered this one every day in mid summer and every other day in cooler weather.

Troubleshooting: After six weeks, the purple salvia was covered up by the coleus. It also suffered from lack of light because I planted another wall basket too close above it. Luckily, the other plants were so pretty that the arrangement still looked great without the purple flowers! Red salvia is taller than the purple and a better choice when surrounded by coleus.

Quantity of Plants: Quantities for this pot size are given on the plant photos (opposite page). See page 12, 14, and 15 for quantities needed for other container sizes and shapes.

Planting Plan: Alternate the begonias, 'Gay's Delight' coleus, and 'Dark Star' coleus, around the side layer. Plant the salvias in the center. Alternate the begonias and coleus again around the top edge.

For product sources, see page 15.

Only one week after planting!

Salvia
(2 plants from 4" pots)
Plant profile: Page 150

'Gay's Delight' Coleus
(4 plants from 4" pots)
Plant profile: Page 140

Wax Begonia
(4 plants from 4" pots)
Plant profile: Page 138

'Dark Star' Coleus
(4 plants from 4" pots)
Plant profile: Page 140

White Liriope, Coleus

16" single basic basket

White was the right color choice for the centerpiece of this arrangement because I wanted something that would really show up from a distance. This container is part of a group of three located a distance down my walkway. White showed well from the beginning of the walk, which was my goal. A darker color would have faded into the background.

The white liriope grass did the trick, acting like a light in a tunnel! Although it is not as tall as the ideal centerpiece - at least 18" - its color made up for its lack of stature. For contrast, I added darker coleus and begonias, complemented by the light *Lysimachia* 'Outback Sunset.'

The coleus is one of the large-leafed types - the Kong series - that stays reasonably small in the sides of containers but grows large enough to really make a splash. The large texture contrasts well with the smaller, textured plants around it.

This basket makes a spectacular show when used as part of a group of three Notice that all three share the same centerpiece. The side and edge plants coordinate but are not identical.

The salvia planted beneath coordinates well with the plants in the baskets on columns.

Cultural Information

Light: Full sun to light shade. Since wax begonias are sold for sun or shade, be sure to choose those that fit your light situation. Most take sun until the temperatures hit the low 90's. The red-leafed varieties take sun in higher temperatures, along with some of the newer, green-leafed types that should be labeled as sun begonias.

Season: Spring through fall for most areas. Also thrives in winter in areas where the temperatures stay above 38 degrees. This plant mix takes temperatures from about 38 degrees to the low 90's in full sun. In light shade, it withstands higher temperatures into the high 90's.

Lifespan: Three to five months in this container. Lives longer in cooler weather, although it lasted four months for me in a hot Georgia summer!

Care: Fertilize on planting day with the slow-release mix described on page 26. Repeat if the leaves look yellowish or washed-out, although the fertilizer should last from six to nine months. Pinch the coleus and the begonias to keep them from getting taller than the liriope centerpiece. Since the centerpiece is so short, you'll need to pinch it at least once a month.

Water: Water when the plants show signs of wilt or the soil feels dry when you push your fingertip up to your second knuckle into the potting mix. I watered this one every day in mid summer (after it was about a month old) and every other day in cooler weather.

Troubleshooting: The large coleus and begonias eventually covered up the *Lysimachia* 'Outback Sunset.' But I didn't mind because the overall arrangement looked so good for so long!

Quantity of Plants: Quantities for this pot size are given on the plant photos (opposite page). See pages 12, 14, and 15 for quantities needed for other container sizes and shapes.

Planting Plan: Alternate begonias, coleus, and *Lysimachia* 'Outback Sunset' around the side layer. Plant the liriope in the center. Alternate the begonias, coleus, and 'Outback Sunset' again around the edge, surrounding the liriope. See pages 18-19 for a full planting demo.

For product sources, see page 15.

Liriope
(1 plant from a 1-gallon pot)
Plant profile: Page 154

Wax Begonia
(8 plants from 4" pots)
Plant profile: Page 138

'Kong Scarlet' Coleus
(8 plants from 4" pots)
Plant profile: Page 150

Lysimachia 'Outback Sunset'
(8 plants from 4" pots)
Plant profile: Page 146

Pink and White

16" double basic basket

T his basket was an experiment that worked - well, most of it, anyway! I planted mature begonias alongside coleus seedlings, risking that the begonias would completely overtake the coleus. But, they grew together quite well. The grass I planted on the top edge, however, was completely smothered by the coleus and begonias. This basket was a success, but it took quite a while to grow in. I much prefer starting with larger plants.

Planting Sequence

Step 1: In the side, layer alternate the begonias with the two colors of coleus.

Step 2: Plant a large penta (or 3 small ones) in the center.

Step 3: Repeat step 1 for the next layer.

Step 4: Plant the edge plants. *(For full planting demo, see page 20-21.)*

Cultural Information

Light: Full sun to light shade. Since wax begonias are sold for sun or shade, be sure to choose those that fit your light situation. Most take sun until the temperatures hit the low 90's. The red-leafed varieties take sun in higher temperatures, along with some of the newer green-leafed types that should be labeled as sun begonias.

Season: Spring through fall for most areas. Also thrives in winter in areas where the temperatures stay above 38 degrees. This plant mix takes temperatures from about 38 degrees to the low 90's in full sun. In light shade, it withstands higher temperatures, into the high 90's.

Lifespan: Four to five months in this container.

Care: Fertilize on planting day with the slow-release mix described on page 26. Repeat if the leaves look yellowish or washed-out, although the fertilizer should last from six to nine months. Pinch the coleus occasionally to keep it from getting leggy. 'Flume' coleus only requires pinching once or twice. Remove the dead flowers from the pentas if you feel energetic!

Water: Water when the plants show signs of wilt or the soil feels dry when you push your fingertip up to your second knuckle into the potting mix. I watered this one every day in mid-summer and every other day in cooler weather.

Troubleshooting: I planted 'Fiber Optic' grass along the top edge (see photo #4, left) for a textural change. It was overtaken by the spreading coleus and begonias. The 'Flume' coleus spread more than most others I have tried. It grew quite dense and seldom requiring pinching.

Quantity of Plants: Quantities for this pot size are given on the plant photos (opposite page). See page 12, 14, and 15 for quantities needed for other container sizes and shapes.

Planting Plan: The begonias and coleus were alternated on both side layers. I should have stuck with the same pattern along the top edge instead of mixing in some 'Fiber Optic' grass!

For product sources, see page 15.

Penta (under butterfly)
(1 plant from a 1-gallon pot)
Plant profile: Page 149

White Wax Begonia
(10 plants from 4" pots)
Plant profile: Page 138

'Flume' Coleus
(10 plants from 4" pots)
Plant profile: Page 140

Pink Wax Begonia
(10 plants from 4" pots)
Plant profile: Page 140

Easy Color!

14" single basic basket

This small basket is one of my favorites of all time. It represents simplicity - both in plant choices and arrangement. What could be simpler than coleus, begonias, and salvia? These winners have been tested and proved by generations of gardeners.

This arrangement is the easiest I know: simply choose a centerpiece you like and surround it with three alternating plants.

I chose two colors of salvia for the centerpiece, purple and red. The purple went in and out of bloom while the red bloomed its heart out for the entire lifespan of this container.

This plant mix works well in cool or warm weather - it even took 97 degrees in our trials.

This basket is part of a display of six that I did in my garden. It is front and center! I coordinated the colors of all the pots but varied the plants. The columns start at 36" tall in front, 42" tall in the middle, and 48" tall in back.

See more about this grouping on pages 120 and 121.

Cultural Information

Light: Full sun to light shade. Since wax begonias are sold for sun or shade, be sure to choose those that fit your light situation. Most take sun until the temperatures hit the low 90's. The red-leafed varieties take sun in higher temperatures, along with some of the newer green-leafed types that should be labeled as sun begonias.

Season: Spring through fall for most areas. Also thrives in winter in areas where the temperatures stay above 38 degrees. This plant mix takes temperatures from about 38 degrees to the low-90's in full sun. In light shade, it withstands higher temperatures into the high 90's.

Lifespan: Four to five months in this container.

Care: Fertilize on planting day with the slow-release mix described on page 26. Repeat if the leaves look yellowish or washed-out, although the fertilizer should last from six to nine months. I pinched the coleus back about every three weeks so that it remained compact and didn't outgrow the salvia centerpiece. Remove the dead flowers from the salvia if you feel energetic!

Water: Water when the plants show signs of wilt or the soil feels dry when you push your fingertip up to your second knuckle into the potting mix. I watered this one every day (after it was about a month old) in mid summer and every other day in cooler weather.

Troubleshooting: I lost one coleus that had been planted in the side. I replaced it, following the instructions on page 27.

Quantity of Plants: Quantities for this pot size are given on the plant photos (opposite page). See page 12, 14, and 15 for quantities needed for other container sizes and shapes.

Planting Plan: The easiest I know! In the side layer, alternate the begonias with the two colors of coleus. Plant the two colors of salvia close together in the center. Repeat the alternating dark coleus, begonia, red/yellow coleus along the top edge. Try to keep the same plant from appearing above itself in the side and edge layers. (For a full planting demo, see page 18-19.)

For product sources, see page 15.

Red Salvia
(2 plants from 4" pots)
Plant profile: Page 150

Purple Salvia
(1 plant from a 4" pot)
Plant profile: Page 150

'Wizard Scarlet' Coleus
(6 plants from 4" pots)
Plant profile: Page 140

Wax Begonia
(5 plants from 4" pots)
Plant profile: Page 138

'Dark Star' Coleus
(5 plants from 4" pots)
Plant profile: Page 140

Flowers, Flowers!

This arrangement is a great choice for flower lovers. And, it attracts lots of butterflies and bumblebees as well. The plant choice would have been simplified had I used just one color of torenia, but I had some left over from another basket, so I used two colors instead.

The torenia (upright) did better surrounded by these plants (begonias and melampodium) than in other combinations I tried. It tended to droop and required cut-backs when surrounded by semi-trailers like creeping Jenny.

Basket on 48" column. Red verbena is planted in the ground underneath.

Cultural Information

Light: Full sun to light shade. Since many wax begonias are grown for shade, be sure to choose those that fit your light situation. Most take sun until the temperatures hit the low 90's. The red-leafed varieties take sun in higher temperatures, along with some of the newer, green-leafed types that should be labeled as sun begonias.

Season: Spring through fall for most areas. Also thrives in winter in areas where the temperatures stay above 50 degrees. This plant mix takes temperatures from about 38 degrees to the low 90's in full sun. In light shade, it withstands higher temperatures into the high 90's.

Lifespan: Four to five months in this container.

Care: Fertilize on planting day with the slow-release mix described on page 26. Repeat if the leaves look yellowish or washed-out, although the fertilizer should last from six to nine months. Repeat if the leaves start looking yellowish or washed-out. Remove the dead flowers from the zinnias if you feel energetic!

Water: Water when the plants show signs of wilt or the soil feels dry when you push your fingertip up to your second knuckle into the potting mix. I watered this one every day in mid-summer (after it was about a month old) and every other day in cooler weather.

Troubleshooting: The zinnia centerpiece got a leaf fungus. I replaced it with a grass when the basket was about three months old.

Quantity of Plants: Quantities for this pot size are given on the plant photos (opposite page). See pages 12, 14, and 15 for quantities needed for other container sizes and shapes.

Planting Plan: Alternate the melampodium, torenia, and begonia in the bottom side layer. Repeat for the top side layer, putting different plants on top of one another. Plant the zinnia centerpiece. Alternate the side-layer plants again along the top edge. (*For a full planting demo, see page 20-21.*)

For product sources, see page 15.

Zinnia
plant from a 1-gallon pot)
Plant profile: Page 154

Torenia, Upright
(6 plants from a 4" pots)
Plant profile: Page 153

Melampodium
(11 plants from a 4" pots)
Plant profile: Page 146

Torenia, Upright
(6 plants from 4" pots)
Plant profile: Page 153

Wax Begonia
(11 plants from 4" pots)
Plant profile: Page 138

Geranium Wall Basket

16" single wall basket

Wall baskets are very useful containers. Place them on an empty wall next to your front door, a column, or a wall on your deck. This arrangement was one of three on my deck. See a photo of the group on page 132-133. The large flower of the geranium centerpiece contrasts well with the smaller-flowered begonia. Two colors of coleus complete the planting.

Planting Sequence

Step 1: In the side layer, alternate the begonias with the two colors of coleus

Step 2: Plant a geranium in the center.

Step 3: Repeat Step 1 around the edge. Be sure to put different plants above each other. *(For full planting demo, see page 22.)*

Cultural Information

Light: Full sun to light shade. Since wax begonias are sold for sun or shade, be sure to choose those that fit your light situation. Most take sun until the temperatures hit the low 90's. The red-leafed varieties take sun in higher temperatures, along with some of the newer green-leafed types that should be labeled as sun begonias.

Season: Spring through fall for most areas. Also thrives in winter in areas where the temperatures stay above 38 degrees. This plant mix takes temperatures from about 38 degrees to the low 90's in full sun. In light shade, it withstands higher temperatures into the high 90's. However, the geraniums will not perform optimally in that much heat.

Lifespan: Two to four months in this container. Plants in small wall baskets live shorter lives than those planted in larger containers.

Care: Fertilize on planting day with the slow-release mix described on page 26. Repeat if the leaves look yellowish or washed-out, although the fertilizer should last from six to nine months. Repeat if the leaves start looking yellowish or washed-out. Pinch the coleus to keep it from getting taller than the geraniums, about every three weeks or so. Remove the dead flowers from the geranium if you feel energetic!

Water: Water when the plants show signs of wilt or the soil feels dry when you push your fingertip up to your second knuckle into the potting mix. I watered this one every day in mid summer and every other day in cooler weather.

Troubleshooting: None. This was a very easy arrangement to plant and grow.

Quantity of Plants: Quantities for this pot size are given on the plant photos (opposite page). See pages 12, 14, and 15 for quantities needed for other container sizes and shapes.

Planting Plan: The begonias and two different coleus were alternated both on the side layer as well as the edge layer. They surround the geranium centerpiece.

For product sources, see page 15.

Geranium
(2 plants from 4" pots)
Plant profile: Page 141

'Dark Star' Coleus
(4 plants from 4" pots)
Plant profile: Page 140

Wax Begonia
(4 plants from 4" pots)
Plant profile: Page 138

Unnamed Coleus
(4 plants from 4" pots)
Plant profile: Page 140

Annuals with Tropicals

20" double basic basket

This basket features coleus, impatiens, and begonias planted in the sides and along the top edge - plants that are not only easy to find but also hard to kill! We had very few fatalities with these dependable plants. The centerpiece is a tropical - mammey croton- that not only looks great but also lasts for the entire growing season.

This is a very simple arrangement - both for beginners as well as experienced gardeners. Simply alternate coleus and impatiens in your favorite colors and you have something that can stop traffic!

These companion baskets mirror the theme of the basket shown to the right. They are underplanted with annual red salvia and white 'Odorata' begonias, a tropical begonias that does well in cool (but not freezing!) weather.

The columns are 48" and 36" tall.

Cultural Information

Light: Full sun to light shade in cooler weather. Impatiens take sun in hot weather but don't like it. They also will drive you crazy with water needs in too much sun and heat, or with longer days in northeastern locations like New Hampshire. Most take sun until the temperatures hit the low 90's. If it's hotter than that, or summer days are quite long where you live, keep them in the shade.

Season: Spring through fall for most areas. Also thrives in winter in areas where the temperatures stay above 33 degrees. This plant mix takes temperatures from about 33 degrees to the low 90's in full sun. In medium shade, it withstands higher temperatures into the high 90's.

Lifespan: Three to five months in this container. Lives longer in cooler weather.

Care: Fertilize on planting day with the slow-release mix described on page 26. Repeat if the leaves look yellowish or washed-out, although the fertilizer should last from six to nine months. Repeat if the leaves look yellowish or washed-out. Pinch the coleus and the impatiens to keep them from getting taller than the croton centerpiece.

Water: Water when the plants show signs of wilt or the soil feels dry when you push your fingertip up to your second knuckle into the potting mix. I watered this one every day in mid summer (after it was about a month old) and every other day to every third day in cooler weather. This basket requires water twice a day in really hot weather.

Troubleshooting: None. This was an easy arrangement.

Quantity of Plants: Quantities for this pot size are given on the plant photos (opposite page). See pages 12, 14, and 15 for quantities needed for other container sizes and shapes.

Planting Plan: Alternate the impatiens and coleus on the side as well as the edge layers. Plant a mammey croton in the center. *(For full planting demo, see pages 20-21.)*

For product sources, see page 15.

Lavender Impatiens
(11 plants from 4" pots)
Plant profile: Page 142

Orange Impatiens
(12 plants from 4" pots)
Plant profile: Page 142

Mammey Croton
(1 plant from a 3-gallon pot)
Plant profile: Page 154

Lime Coleus
(12 plants from 4" pots)
Plant profile: Page 140

Summer Pinks

20" double basic basket

What a great combination for hot summer days! The large leaves of the caladium centerpiece stand out well against the other, smaller-leaved plants. And the dragon wing begonias blend beautifully with the two different coleus.

Dragon wing begonias are one of my favorite container plants. They are difficult to find in 4" pots because they don't look too good when they are so small. However, if you see any, I highly recommend trying them. They are showier than the more common wax begonias and unusual as well.

Another similar basket hanging on my gazebo. I like to hang identical baskets on this gazebo because it is rather formal and symmetrical. However, on informal porches or decks, different baskets work well together.

Cultural Information

Light: Light shade is ideal.

Season: Spring through fall for most warmer areas. This plant mix takes temperatures from about 62 degrees to the low 90's. In a bit more shade, it withstands temperatures into the mid 90's.

Lifespan: Three to five months in this container.

Care: Fertilize on planting day with the slow-release mix described on page 26. Repeat if the leaves look yellowish or washed-out, although the fertilizer should last from six to nine months. Pinch the coleus and the begonias to keep them from getting taller than the liriope centerpiece. Since the centerpiece is so short, you'll need to pinch at least once a month.

Water: Water when the plants show signs of wilt or the soil feels dry when you push your fingertip up to your second knuckle into the potting mix. I watered this one every day (after it was about a month old) in mid summer and every other day in cooler weather.

Troubleshooting: The 'Wizard Rose' coleus has not been doing well in the last year or so. Be sure it has a warranty if you buy it. The torenia started to disappear after a month or so, but I really enjoyed those blue flowers while they lasted!

Quantity of Plants: Quantities for this size pot size are given on the plant photos (opposite page). See pages 12, 14, and 15 for quantities needed for other container sizes and shapes.

Planting Plan: Easy. Alternate the begonias, coleus, and torenia on the side as well as the edge layers. Plant the caladiums in the center. *(For full planting demo, see paged 20-21.)*

For product sources, see page 15.

'orida Fantasy' Caladium
(3 plants from 4.5" pots)
Plant Profile: Page 139

'Painted Pink' Coleus
(8 plants from 4.5" pots)
Plant Profile: Page 140

Upright Torenia
(8 plants from 4.5" pots)
Plant Profile: Page 153

Dragon Wing Begonia
(9 plants from 4.5" pots)
Plant Profile: Page 138

'Wizard Rose' Coleus
(9 plants from 4.5" pots)
Plant Profile: Page 140

Easy and Gorgeous!

16" imperial planter

It's a good idea to start simple when your are planting your first few instant containers. This basket is a great inspiration for beginners because it is not only very easy to plant but also gorgeous after it is done. You can't get much better than that!

Dragon wing begonias are one of my favorite container plants. They are difficult to find in 4" pots because they don't look too good when they are so small. However, if you see any, I highly recommend trying them. They are showier than the more-common wax begonias, and unusual as well.

If you can't find them and like this look, substitute wax begonias. They are almost always available in red.

Another similar basket with pink dragon wing begonias, lime coleus, and a Perilla Magilla for the centerpiece.

Cultural Information

Light: Light shade is ideal.

Season: Spring through fall for most warmer areas. This plant mix takes temperatures from about 38 degrees to the low-90's. In a bit more shade, it withstands temperatures into the mid-90's.

Lifespan: Three to five months in this container.

Care: Fertilize on planting day with the slow-release mix described on page 26. Repeat if the leaves look yellowish or washed-out, although the fertilizer should last from six to nine months. Pinch the coleus and the begonias to keep them from getting taller than the croton centerpiece. Since the centerpiece is so short, you'll need to pinch at least once a month.

Water: Water when the plants show signs of wilt or the soil feels dry when you push your fingertip into the potting mix - up to your second knuckle. I watered this one every day (after it was about a month old) in mid summer and every other day in cooler weather.

Troubleshooting: No problems. This was a wonderful, trouble-free basket.

Quantity of Plants: Quantities for this size pot are given on the plant photos (opposite page). See pages 12, 14, and 15 for quantities needed for other container sizes and shapes.

Planting Plan: Easy. Alternate the begonias and coleus on both side layers as well as along the edge layers. Plant the mammey croton in the center. *(For full planting demo, see pages 20-21.)*

For product sources, see page 15.

Mammey Croton
(1 plant from a 3-gallon pot)
Plant Profile: Page 154

Dragon Wing Begonia
(15 plants from 4.5" pots)
Plant Profile: Page 138

Coleus 'Mardi Gras'
(15 plants from 4.5" pots)
Plant Profile: Page 140

All Coleus

16" imperial planter

Coleus is one of the best plants for container planting. It offers constant color for very little care. The variety of colors, sizes, and shapes is amazing and increasing every day. This arrangement is all coleus. Friends have told me that it resembles a quilt.

I used 'Crime Scene' coleus as the centerpiece because it grows taller than most other coleus. The sides feature three different coleus, all with different patterns and leaf sizes.

Cultural Information

Light: Light shade is ideal.

Season: Spring through fall for most warmer areas. This plant mix takes temperatures from about 38 degrees to the low 90's. In a bit more shade, it withstands temperatures into the mid 90's.

Lifespan: Three to five months in this container.

Care: Fertilize on planting day with the slow-release mix described on page 26. Repeat if the leaves look yellowish or washed-out, although the fertilizer should last from six to nine months. Pinch the coleus as needed to keep it even and full.

Water: Water when the plants show signs of wilt or the soil feels dry when you push your fingertip up to your second knuckle into the potting mix. I watered this one every day in mid summer (after it was about a month old) and every other day in cooler weather.

Troubleshooting: No problems. This was a wonderful, trouble-free basket.

Quantity of Plants: Quantities for this pot size are given on the plant photos (opposite page). See pages 12, 14, and 15 for quantities needed for other container sizes and shapes.

Planting Plan: Easy. Alternate the coleus for both side layers as well as along the tope edge. Plant the 'Crime Scene' coleus in the center. *(For full planting demo, see pages 20-21.)*

A companion basket with a different mix of the same colors of coleus.

For product sources, see page 15.

Coleus 'Crime Scene'
(1 plant from a 1-gallon pot)
Plant Profile: Page 140

Coleus 'Red Trailing Queen'
(10 plants from 4.5" pots)
Plant Profile: Page 140

Coleus 'Wizard Golden'
(10 plants from 4.5" pots)
Plant Profile: Page 140

Coleus 'Freckles'
(10 plants from 4.5" pots)
Plant Profile: Page 140

Shrimp Plant Centerpiece

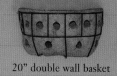

20" double wall basket

The golden shrimp plant used as the centerpiece of this arrangement is a fabulous and underused container plant. It blooms in temperatures from 38 to 95 degrees, living for years in areas without freezes. It will last throughout any long growing season, blooming constantly.

This plant coordinates well with the coleus and dragon wing begonias. Wax begonias would work, too, if it is difficult to find the dragon wings in small enough containers to fit in the side holes.

This double wall basket is the largest wall basket in this line. The extra size allows the plants to grow for a longer period than the smaller baskets. This arrangement lasted for a full five months in this large container. If the same plants were planted in a 16" or 20" single wall basket, you could expect three to four months of life.

A companion basket with the same color scheme.

Cultural Information

Light: Light shade is ideal. Takes more sun in cooler areas. The shrimp plant will suffer in full sun and 95 degree temperatures!

Season: Spring through fall for most warmer areas. This plant mix takes temperatures from about 38 degrees to the mid 90's. It works all year in areas that stay within those bounds.

Lifespan: Five months in this container.

Care: Fertilize on planting day with the slow-release mix described on page 26. Repeat if the leaves look yellowish or washed-out, although the fertilizer should last from six to nine months. Pinch the coleus as needed to keep it even and full.

Water: Water when the plants show signs of wilt or the soil feels dry when you push your fingertip up to your second knuckle into the potting mix. I watered this one every day in mid summer (after it was about a month old) and every other day in cooler weather.

Troubleshooting: Pinch back the coleus every month or so to keep them full.

Quantity of Plants: Quantities for this pot size are given on the plant photos (opposite page). See pages 12, 14, and 15 for quantities needed for other container sizes and shapes.

Planting Plan: Easy. Alternate the coleus and begonias for both side layers as well as along the top edge. Plant the shrimp plant in the center. *(For full planting demo, see page 22.)*

For product sources, see page 15.

Golden Shrimp Plant
(2 plants from 1gallon pots)
Plant Profile: Page 151

'Dark Star' Coleus
(6 plants from 4.5" pots)
Plant Profile: Page 140

Dragon Wing Begonia
(6 plants from 4.5" pots)
Plant Profile: Page 138

'Gay's Delight' Coleus
(6 plants from 4.5" pots)
Plant Profile: Page 140

Easy Combo

20" double basic basket

Coleus surrounding a grass centerpiece is one of the easiest combos I know. It is especially easy if the grass you choose is tall enough to naturally grow larger than the coleus. That natural height difference minimizes the need to pinch the coleus to keep it smaller than the grass.

I used many different coleus in these trials and was quite happy to learn that I don't have to worry so much about their ultimate height. Since coleus vary so much in size when planted in the ground, I had initially thought that I would have to be quite careful to choose container companions that were similar in natural height. This was not the case, however. I used large 'Kong' coleus right next to smaller varieties. A little pinching kept the arrangements quite even.

A companion basket with a different mix of the same colors of coleus.

Cultural Information

Light: Light shade to full sun.

Season: Spring through fall for most warmer areas. This plant mix takes temperatures from about 38 degrees to the low 90's. In a bit more shade, it withstands temperatures into the mid 90's.

Lifespan: Four to five months in this container.

Care: Fertilize on planting day with the slow-release mix described on page 26. Repeat if the leaves look yellowish or washed-out, although the fertilizer should last from six to nine months. Pinch the coleus as needed to keep it even and full.

Water: Water when the plants show signs of wilt or the soil feels dry when you push your fingertip up to your second knuckle into the potting mix. I watered this one every day (after it was about a month old) in mid summer and every other day in cooler weather.

Troubleshooting: No problems. This was a wonderful, trouble-free basket.

Quantity of Plants: Quantities for this pot size are given on the plant photos (opposite page). See pages 12, 14, and 15 for quantities needed for other container sizes and shapes.

Planting Plan: Easy. Alternate the coleus for both side layers as well as along the top edge. Plant the grass in the center. *(For full planting demo, see pages 20-21.)*

For product sources, see page 15.

Red Fountain Grass
(1 plant from a 3-gallon pot)
Plant Profile: Page 142

Coleus 'Red Trailing Queen'
(12 plants from 4.5" pots)
Plant Profile: Page 140

Coleus 'Wizard Golden'
(12 plants from 4.5" pots)
Plant Profile: Page 140

Coleus 'Painted Lady'
(11 plants from 4.5" pots)
Plant Profile: Page 140

'Matrix Sunrise' Pansies

30" window box

This window box has more coco-fiber showing than any other arrangement in this book. Whereas most of the containers in this book were planted in spring, this one was planted in fall. The cool weather that followed caused the pansies to grow much slower than the plants in the spring containers. It still had the coco-fiber showing two months after planting. But the 'Matrix Sunrise' pansies were so pretty that the container became an asset to that side of my home.

The bok choy in the center is a vegetable that takes some winter cold. It gets quite tall, however, and requires some trimming.

I tested many different types of pansies. The 'Matrix Sunrise' did particularly well.

Window boxes can be displayed on patios as well as under windows. This one is resting on Pot Toes to lift is off the bricks. Patios stay cleaner if containers are raised. See page 14 for more information.

Cultural Information

Light: Full sun is ideal.

Season: Pansies thrive in the cool season, in spring in most areas and are used commonly in winter in zone 7 further south. Bok choy and this ti plant take cold down to about 28 degrees. I moved this box indoors when the temperature went under 28 degrees.

Lifespan: Five to six months in this container.

Care: Fertilize on planting day with a slow-release mix described on page 26. Repeat if the leaves look yellowish or washed-out, although the fertilizer should last from six to nine months. Trim the bok choy if it gets leggy.

Water: I planted this container for winter use. Not much water was needed. But be sure to check it! Water when the potting mix is dry to the touch. Be sure to water it before cold spells, which really dry out containers.

Troubleshooting: No problems. This was a wonderful, trouble-free basket.

Quantity of Plants: Quantities for this pot size are given on the plant photos (opposite page). See pages 12, 14, and 15 for quantities needed for other container sizes and shapes.

Planting Plan: Easy. Plant the 'Matrix Sunrise' pansies in the sides. Plant the bok choy and ti plants in the top. Plant the rest of the pansies around the top edge. *(For full planting demo, see page 23.)*

For product sources, see page 15.

Ti Plant
(6 plants from 4.5" pots)
Plant Profile: Page 152

Chinese Mustard, Bok Choy
(1 plant from a 1-gallon pot)
Plant Profile: Page 154

Pansy 'Matrix Sunrise'
(16 plants from 4.5" pots)
Plant Profile: Page 148

Tricky Verbena

20" double basic basket

Although I had better luck with verbena than petunias, they were a bit tricky as well. The upright verbena didn't do well at all, either in the sides or planted in the top of the basket. Trailing verbena (planted in this basket) did better, even when planted in the sides; however, the blooms were not as dependable as some of the really high performers, like begonias and impatiens. I will keep using trailing verbena, however, because I really like the way it looks!

The colors in this basket are wonderful - different shades of purple. This color scheme was very popular in our trial gardens. I like to add some variegated leaves to the purple mix, shown here with the lamium 'White Nancy'.

The basket would have a lot more flowers in cooler locations than Florida - in Oregon or Colorado, for example. The plants grow slower and denser in cooler weather, producing many more flowers.

A companion basket with pink flowers.

Cultural Information

Light: Light shade to full sun is ideal.

Season: Varies, based on where you live. Plant this mix when your temperatures range from 45 degrees to about 80 degrees. The Mona lavender stops blooming in hot weather.

Lifespan: Four to five months in this container.

Care: Fertilize on planting day with the slow-release mix described on page 26. Repeat if the leaves look yellowish or washed-out, although the fertilizer should last from six to nine months. Pinch the lamium as needed to keep it even and full. It will trail if you leave it alone, and you may prefer it that way.

Water: Water when the plants show signs of wilt or the soil feels dry when you push your fingertip up to your second knuckle into the potting mix. I watered this one every three days (after it was about a month old).

Troubleshooting: No problems. This was a wonderful, trouble-free basket.

Quantity of Plants: Quantities for this pot size are given on the plant photos (opposite page). See pages 12, 14, and 15 for quantities needed for other container sizes and shapes.

Planting Plan: Easy. Alternate the melampodium, petunias, and mint for both side layers as well as along the top edge. Plant the Mona lavender in the center. *(For full planting demo, see pages 20-21.)*

For product sources, see page 15.

Mona Lavender
(plant from a 1-gallon pot)
Plant Profile: Page 147

Lamium
'White Nancy'
(9 plants from 4.5" pots)
Plant Profile: Page 145

Supertunia (Petunia)
'Mini Rose Veined'
(9 plants from 4.5" pots)
Plant Profile: Page 150

Superbena (Verbena)
'Large Lilac Blue'
(9 plants from 4.5" pots)
Plant Profile: Page 155

Supertunia (Petunia)
'Royal Velvet'
(8 plants from 4.5" pots)
Plant Profile: Page 150

Short-Lived Beauty

16" imperial planter

At one point during my years of trials with these baskets, I had about 30 in the garden at once. I had some friends over and asked which was their favorite. The majority liked this one the best. The only problem was it did not last as long as I would have liked - only two months.

Lobelia has been side-planted for years in England with no problems. But it didn't last too long for me, even though I planted it when the weather was fairly cool. Since it is one of my favorite plants (and a hanging basket classic), I will keep trying!

The Jacob's coat suffered the same problem. It died after about two months.

Cultural Information

Light: Full sun to light shade in cool weather.

Season: Lobelia is a cool weather plant, preferring temperatures under 85 degrees. The rest of the plants in the arrangement take much more heat.

Lifespan: Two months in this container.

Care: Fertilize on planting day with a slow-release mix described on page 26. Repeat if the leaves look yellowish or washed-out, although the fertilizer should last from six to nine months. Pinch the dead flowers off the salvia if you feel energetic!

Water: Water when the plants show signs of wilt or the soil feels dry when you push your fingertip up to your second knuckle into the potting mix. I watered this one every three days (it was cool at the time!).

Troubleshooting: Lobelia and Jacob's coat were short-lived; they lasted only about two months.

Quantity of Plants: Quantities for this pot size are given on the plant photos (opposite page). See pages 12, 14, and 15 for quantities needed for other container sizes and shapes.

Planting Plan: Easy. Alternate the lobelia, Jacob's coat, and begonias for both side layers as well as along the top edge. Plant the salvia in the center. (*For full planting demo, see pages 20-21.*)

This basket has a similar look but lasted twice as long. The yellow Lysimachia 'Outback Sunset' and the purple 'Dark Star' coleus like being planted in the sides better than the Jacob's coat and lobelia, shown right.

For product sources, see page 15.

Salvia
(3 plants from 1-gallon pots)
Plant Profile: Page 150

Jacob's Coat
(10 plants from 4.5" pots)
Plant Profile: Page 154

Wax Begonia
(10 plants from 4.5" pots)
Plant Profile: Page 138

Lobelia
(10 plants from 4.5" pots)
Plant Profile: Page 154

Tricky but Gorgeous!

20" double basic basket

I planted this basket after I had already had a hard time with lobelia. And finally, it worked! The lobelia 'Laguna Sky Blue' did quite well in this basket. The trailing verbena also stayed in bloom longer than any I had tested before. I'll still call this one tricky because I have had problems with some of the plants in the past; but overall, it was a real winner!

The grass contrasts quite well with the flowers. The size difference between the larger verbena flower and the smaller lobelia also adds to the interest of this arrangement.

The lime coleus works well because it adds some light color to contrast with the darker leaves of the other plants.

Look at the difference between empty basket (above) and the planted basket (opposite). I photographed the 'after' immediately after planting!

Cultural Information

Light: Light shade to full sun.

Season: Lobelia is a cool weather plant, preferring temperatures under 85 degrees. The rest of the plants in the arrangement take much more heat. Do not use this combination in less than 38 degrees.

Lifespan: Four to five months in this container.

Care: Fertilize on planting day with the slow-release mix described on page 26. Repeat if the leaves look yellowish or washed-out, although the fertilizer should last from six to nine months. Pinch the coleus as needed to keep it even and full.

Water: Water when the plants show signs of wilt or the soil feels dry up to your second knuckle when you push your fingertip into the potting mix. I watered this one every day (after it was about a month old) in mid summer and every other day in cooler weather.

Troubleshooting: No problems. This was a wonderful, trouble-free basket.

Quantity of Plants: Quantities for this pot size are given on the plant photos (opposite page). See pages 12, 14, and 15 for quantities needed for other container sizes and shapes.

Planting Plan: Easy. Alternate the verbena, lobelia, and coleus for both side layers as well as along the top edge. Plant the *Juncus* in the center. *(For full planting demo, see pages 20-21.)*

For product sources, see page 15.

This photo was taken immediately after planting!

Juncus 'Quartz Creek'
(1 plant from a 3-gallon pot)
Plant Profile: Page 145

Trailing Verbena
(12 plants from 4.5" pots)
Plant Profile: Page 155

Coleus 'Gay's Delight'
(12 plants from 4.5" pots)
Plant Profile: Page 140

Lobelia 'Laguna Sky Blue'
(11 plants from 4.5" pots)
Plant Profile: Page 154

Tricky Petunias

20" double basic basket

Petunias are one of my favorite plants for hanging baskets. They are quite tricky for side-planting, however. Many petunias I bought without cultivar labels (their label just said 'Petunia') died when planted in the side. Others with the same labeling did fine. Two cultivars did well all the time: The 'Supertunias' from Proven Winners and the 'Easy Wave' petunias from Ball Seed. So, use petunias in the sides at your own risk!

This basket was grown in the winter in Florida. It would work in most of the country when the temperatures are between 45 degrees and 80 degrees. The mix does not do well in hot weather because the Mona lavender centerpiece doesn't bloom in too much heat.

The basket would have a lot more flowers in cooler locations than Florida - in Oregon or Colorado, for example. The plants grow slower and denser in cooler weather, producing many more flowers.

But it was wonderful to have this cool-weather look in my not-so-cool garden!

A companion basket with similar flowers.

Cultural Information

Light: Light shade to full sun is ideal.

Season: Varies, based on where you live. Plant this mix when your temperatures range from 45 degrees to about 80 degrees. The Mona lavender stops blooming in hot weather.

Lifespan: Four to five months in this container.

Care: Fertilize on planting day with a slow-release mix. Repeat if the leaves look yellowish or washed-out. Pinch the mint as needed to keep it even and full. It will trail if you leave it alone, and you may prefer it that way.

Water: Water when the plants show signs of wilt or the soil feels dry when you push your fingertip up to your second knuckle into the potting mix. I watered this one every three days (after it was about a month old).

Troubleshooting: No problems. This was a wonderful, trouble-free basket.

Quantity of Plants: Quantities for this pot size are given on the plant photos (opposite page). See pages 12, 14, and 15 for quantities needed for other container sizes and shapes.

Planting Plan: Easy. Alternate the melampodium, petunias, and mint for both side layers as well as along the top edge. Plant the Mona lavender in the center. *(For full planting demo, see page 20-21.)*

For product sources, see page 15.

Mona Lavender
(plant from a 1-gallon pot)
Plant Profile: Page 141

Melampodium
(9 plants from 4.5" pots)
Plant Profile: Page 140

**Supertunia (Petunia)
'Mini Rose Veined'**
(9 plants from 4.5" pots)
Plant Profile: Page 144

**Plectranthus Variegata
or Variegated Mint**
(8 plants from 4.5" pots)
Plant Profile: Page 141

Petunia
(8 plants from 4.5" pots)
Plant Profile: Page 144

Chapter 4

Designs with Trailing Plants

Creeping Jenny
Plant Profile: Page 144

Sweet Potato
Plant Profile: Page 151

Lamium
Plant Profile: Page 145

Vinca Vine
Plant Profile: Page 155

Syngonium
Plant Profile: Page 155

Trailing Torenia
Plant Profile: Page 152

The top ten trailing plants are shown on these two pages.

The long trailers (sweet potato, ivy, vinca vine, and long petunias*) work best in striped arrangements, described to the right.

Creeping Jenny, lamium, syngonium, trailing torenia, variegated mint, and *Lysimachia* 'Outback Sunset', and short petunias* work in both striped and 1-2-3 designs. They grow slowly, and maintain the characteristics of mounding plants if they are trimmed. Read this chapter to learn these and other ideas that I discovered along the way!

Some varieties of petunias trail 2 ot 3 feet (long peturnias), while others remain quite short (short petunias).

Many planting patterns are shown in this chapter. But it is the only chapter that includes striped designs.

<u>Characteristics of striped designs</u>

❀ Alternate between two and four different plants around both the sides and the edge.

❀ Place the same plants above one another for a vertical, striped look. (See the next page for a demo.)

❀ Plant a contrasting center-piece.

<u>Benefits of striped designs</u>

❀ Even growth habit

❀ Easy to design and plant

❀ Great for long, trailing plants. Since you are planting the same plants above one another, a long trailer won't smother a smaller, mounding plant that is growing beneath it.

Above: Basket on a column that includes both dark purple and lime green sweet potato vine, New Guinea Impatiens, lime coleus, and purple pentas as the centerpiece.

Petunias
Plant Profile: Page 150

Ivy
Plant Profile: Page 144

Variegated Mint
Plant Profile: Page 147

Lysimachia 'Outback Sunset'
Plant Profile: Page 146

Striped Design

16" single wall basket

This wall pot was an instant success. I found long, trailing, creeping Jenny, which is unusual. Since it was so long, I placed it in the side and then on the edge directly above, so that the creeping Jenny and the coleus formed a vertical, striped pattern (see figure 3). Had I planted the long, creeping Jenny above a coleus, it would have smothered it.

Planting Sequence

Step 1: Alternate the coleus and the creeping Jenny around the side layer.

Step 2: Plant the 'Kong' coleus in the middle.

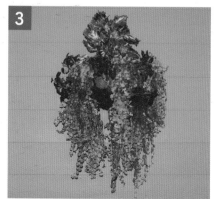

Step 3: Repeat Step 1 around the edge. Be sure to put the same plants above each other. *(For full planting demo, see page 22.)*

Cultural Information

Light: Full sun to light shade.

Season: Spring through fall for most areas. Also thrives in winter in areas where the temperatures stay above 38 degrees. This plant mix takes temperatures from about 38 degrees to the low 90's in full sun. In light shade, it withstands higher temperatures into the high 90's.

Lifespan: Two to four months in this container. Plants in small wall baskets live shorter lives than those planted in larger containers.

Care: Fertilize on planting day with the slow-release mix described on page 26. Repeat if the leaves look yellowish or washed-out, although the fertilizer should last from six to nine months. Pinch the coleus to keep it from getting leggy.

Water: Water when the plants show signs of wilt or the soil feels dry when you push your fingertip up to your second knuckle into the potting mix. I watered this one every day in mid summer and every other day in cooler weather.

Troubleshooting: I started with a different centerpiece, a 'Kong Mosaic' as shown in the photos, left. After a week, it was a bit leggy. Since I had a really full 'Kong Scarlet,' I planted it instead of the first centerpiece, as you can see in the opposite photo.

Quantity of Plants: Quantities for this pot size are given on the plant photos (opposite page). See page 12, 14, and 15 for quantities needed for other container sizes and shapes.

Planting Plan: I call this arrangement 'striping' because you place the same plants above each other in the side and edge layers, like vertical stripes. I use striping when I am working with long, trailing plants, so the trailer doesn't smother the plant underneath it. Creeping Jenny is quite versatile, however. If I am working with more compact specimen, I will alternate the same way I use a mounding plant - with different plants above each other. Creeping Jenny is not an aggressive trailer and doesn't smother the plants beneath it unless it is really long when you plant it.

For product sources, see page 15.

Only one week after planting!

Unnamed Coleus
(6 plants from 4" pots)
Plant profile: Page 140

'Kong' Coleus
(1 plant from a 1-gallon pot)
Plant profile: Page 140

Creeping Jenny
(6 plants from 4" pots)
Plant profile: Page 144

Small Window Box, Big Impact

24" window box

This non-descript window next to my garage came alive with the simple addition of this small window box. The dark colors of the sweet potato vine and the 'Dark Star' coleus mirror the dark shutters. The trailing habit of the vine added an additional accent below the edge of the window. Notice how I only used three of these aggressive vines for a big show in this arrangement.

Planting Sequence

Step 1: Alternate the sweet potato, begonia, and *Lysimachia* 'Outback Sunset' in the side planting holes. Notice how the sweet potato is planted on each end and in the center. Since it will grow quite long, this even spacing will keep the arrangement even.

Step 2: Plant a grass in the center (See trouble shooting).

Step 3: Alternate the begonia, dark coleus, and *Lysimachia* 'Outback Sunset' on the edge. Notice that no sweet potatoes are planted on the edge. *(For full planting instructions, see page 23)*

Cultural Information

Light: Full sun to light shade. Since wax begonias are sold for sun or shade, be sure to choose those that fit your light situation. Most take sun until the temperatures hit the low 90's. The red-leafed varieties take sun in higher temperatures, along with some of the newer, green-leafed types that should be labeled as sun begonias.

Season: Spring through fall for most areas. Also thrives in winter in areas where the temperatures stay above 38 degrees. This plant mix takes temperatures from about 38 degrees to the low-90's in full sun. In light shade, it withstands higher temperatures, into the high 90's.

Lifespan: Three to four months in this container.

Care: Fertilize on planting day with the slow-release mix described on page 26. Repeat if the leaves look yellowish or washed-out, although the fertilizer should last from six to nine months. Pinch the coleus to keep it from getting leggy. Trim the sweet potato as needed to keep it from taking over your house!

Water: Water when the plants show signs of wilt or the soil feels dry when you push your fingertip up to your second knuckle into the potting mix. I watered this one every day in mid summer and every other day in cooler weather.

Troubleshooting: Notice that the centerpiece in the photos shown left is different from the photo shown right. I tried an experiment on the original centerpiece and killed it. It was a very full grass in a 3-gallon pot. I took a sharp saw and cut it in two in an attempt to fit it into this box. It died, and I replaced it with the *Juncus* grass shown to the right. How will I learn unless I experiment?

Quantity of Plants: Quantities for this pot size are given on the plant photos (opposite page). See pages 12, 14, and 15 for quantities needed for other container sizes and shapes.

Planting Plan: Usually, I plant the same plants in the sides as around the edge. This time, I changed. The side layer includes the dark sweet potato, and the edge layer includes dark coleus instead. I was concerned that planting sweet potatoes on the edge would smother the plants below.

For product sources, see page 15.

Sweet Potato
plants from 4" pots)
ant profile: Page 151

Wax Begonia
(5 plants from 4" pots)
Plant profile: Page 138

Juncus **Grass**
(1 plant from a 1-gallon pot)
Plant profile: Page 145

Dark Star Coleus
(2 plants from 4" pots)
Plant profile: Page 140

**Lysimachia
'Outback Sunset'**
(4 plants from 4" pots)
Plant profile: Page 146

Great Basket on Post!

20" double basic basket

Lime green and burgundy proved to be a very popular color scheme in my trial garden because this arrangement was many people's favorite. It was also reasonably easy to maintain.

Planting Sequence

Step 1: Place sweet potato vines in 3 opposite holes on the bottom layer. Alternate coleus and torenia in the other holes.

Step 2: Plant three small ti plants in the center.
Step 3: Alternate sweet potato, coleus, torenia, and creeping Jenny on the top side layer. Be sure to place the sweet potato opposite its bottom layer position.

Step 4: Alternate coleus, torenia, and creeping Jenny around the top edge. This photo was taken 3 weeks after planting. (*For full planting demo, see page 20-21.*)

Cultural Information

Light: Full sun to light shade.

Season: Spring through fall for most areas. Also thrives in winter in areas where the temperatures stay above 40 degrees. This plant mix takes temperatures from about 40 degrees to the low 90's in full sun. In light shade, it withstands higher temperatures into the high 90's.

Lifespan: Four to five months in this container.

Care: Fertilize on planting day with the slow-release fertilizer. Repeat if the leaves start looking yellowish or washed-out. Pinch the coleus to keep it from getting taller than the ti plants, about every three weeks or so. Trim the sweet potato as needed to keep it from taking over the arrangement - about every two weeks or so.

Water: Water when the plants show signs of wilt or the soil feels dry when you push your fingertip up to your second knuckle into the potting mix. I watered this one every two to three days in mid summer. It was planted in light shade. If it had been in the sun, it would have required daily watering when the weather was hot.

Troubleshooting: The container shown at bottom left showed all plants that were planted. The picture was taken three weeks after planting. Look at the difference with the one shown at right, which was two months old. The large coleus and sweet potato vine dominated the arrangement, with the less aggressive torenia and creeping Jenny barely visible. I really liked this one, however, because it looked great for so long.

Quantity of Plants: Quantities for this pot size are given on the plant photos (opposite page). See page 12, 14, and 15 for quantities needed for other container sizes and shapes.

Planting Plan: Whereas most of my arrangements are fairly simple, this one was quite complicated. It is spelled out in the "Planting Sequence" shown left. Basically, I just played with the plants, placing them opposite each other on the different levels to see how it would grow. It is fun to sometimes forego the 'definite pattern' and just do your own thing!

For product sources, see page 15.

Sweet Potato
(6 plants from 4" pots)
Plant profile: Page 151

'Kong Scarlet' Coleus
(10 plants from 4" pots)
Plant profile: Page 140

Creeping Jenny
(8 plants from 4" pots)
Plant profile: Page 144

Ti Plant
(3 plants from 4" pots)
Plant profile: Page 140

Torenia Catalina 'Midnight Blue'
(11 plants from 4" pots)
Plant profile: Page 152

Black and White

Black and white make a dramatic and eye-catching combination. So eye-catching, in fact, that it brought lots of 'oohs and aahs' from our trial garden visitors. It offered the additional benefit of being extremely easy. This basket filled out quickly and thrived throughout a long, hot summer.

Caladiums make superb centerpieces. Their large-leaf texture contrasts well with smaller leaves and grasses. They are quite dependable provided the temperatures are over 64 degrees.

Cultural Information

Light: Light to medium shade.

Season: Spring through fall for most areas. Most caladiums require temperatures of over 64 degrees to grow.

Lifespan: Three to five months in this container.

Care: Fertilize on planting day with a slow-release fertilizer. Repeat if the leaves start looking yellowish or washed-out. Trim the sweet potato back so it doesn't take over the other plants.

Water: Water when the plants show signs of wilt or the soil feels dry up to your second knuckle when you push your fingertip into the potting mix. I watered this about every three days because it was in shade.

Troubleshooting: I spent a lot of money for the black mondo grass that barely shows above the variegated mint. The arrangement would have looked just as good without it!

Quantity of Plants: Quantities for this pot size are given on the plant photos (opposite page). See page 12, 14, and 15 for quantities needed for other container sizes and shapes.

Planting Plan: On the side layer, alternate sweet potato, variegated mint, and coleus. Plant the caladium in the center. Repeat the side plants around the edge. I added a black mondo in the center of the edge, but it's not worth the trouble and money because it was hardly visible after the plants had grown just a little!

Stick with a theme! I learned that lesson when I started to mix the black and white arrangement with other colors. Doesn't it look better over white begonias (right) than it does over mixed salvia (above)?

For product sources, see page 15.

Sweet Potato
(5 plants from 4" pots)
Plant profile: Page 151

Caladium
(1 plant from a 6" pot)
Plant profile: Page 139

Black Mondo Grass
(2 plants from 4" pots)
Plant profile: Page 154

Variegated Mint
(6 plants from 4" pots)
Plant profile: Page 147

'Dark Star' Coleus
(5 plants from 4" pots)
Plant profile: Page 154

Easy and Beautiful!

20" double basic basket

I used this basket to trial 'Easy Wave' petunias. Since so many petunias had died on me when they were planted in the sides, I was thrilled when the 'Easy Waves' did so well. And, they lasted a long time in very hot weather.

I planted periwinkles around the top edge, which I didn't like. They grew unevenly, sticking out awkwardly here and there. It would have been a better idea to stick with the successful petunias and begonias around the top edge. But, once again, you never know until you try something!

As usual, the grass in the center did beautifully. The fuzzy things at the tips are actually the flowers and seeds. They appear near the end of the summer season and add quite a bit to an arrangement.

This pot is mounted on a 48" post.

Wall pot planted with 'Easy Wave' petunias. This photo was taken about a month after planting.

Cultural Information

Light: Light shade to full sun is ideal. Since wax begonias are sold for sun or shade, be sure to choose those that fit your light situation. Most take sun until the temperatures hit the low 90's. The red-leafed varieties take sun in higher temperatures, along with some of the newer, green-leafed types that should be labeled as sun begonias.

Season: Spring through fall for most warmer areas. This plant mix takes temperatures from about 40 degrees to the low 90's. In a bit more shade, it withstands temperatures into the mid 90's.

Lifespan: Four to five months in this container.

Care: Fertilize on planting day with the slow-release mix described on page 26. Repeat if the leaves look yellowish or washed-out, although the fertilizer should last from six to nine months. That's it! This is a really easy design.

Water: Water when the plants show signs of wilt or the soil feels dry when you push your fingertip up to your second knuckle into the potting mix. I watered this one every day (after it was about a month old) in mid summer and every other day in cooler weather.

Troubleshooting: I wasn't crazy about the periwinkles along the top edge. This basket would look better with the begonias and petunias repeated along the top edge.

Quantity of Plants: Quantities for this pot size are given on the plant photos (opposite page). See page 12, 14, and 15 for quantities needed for other container sizes and shapes.

Planting Plan: Easy. Alternate the begonias and petunias in both side layers. Plant the grass in the center. Plant periwinkles around the grass along the top edge. (*For full planting demo, see pages 20-21.*)

For product sources, see page 15.

Fountain Grass
(1 plant from a 3-gallon pot)
Plant Profile: Page 142

Wax Begonia
(10 plants from 4.5" pots)
Plant Profile: Page 138

'Easy Wave' Petunias
(11 plants from 4.5" pots)
Plant Profile: Page 150

Periwinkles
(14 plants from 4.5" pots)
Plant Profile: Page 155

Easy Wall Pot

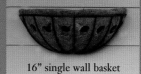

16" single wall basket

While some people prefer a riot of different colors in an arrangement, others like monochromatic (shades of the same color) schemes. This mix of plants in the peach family contrast well with the light green wall behind them.

The *Syngonium* 'Neon' was quite a surprise because I expected it to trail. It didn't, staying quite compact during its entire four month lifespan. Eventually, it does trail, but it is a slow grower, so expect it to behave more like a mounding plant if you use it for only one season.

This arrangement was very easy to care for because it did not need much pinching or grooming. And, I had it in a shady location, which greatly diminished its need for water.

Tricolor dracaena is another great companion for this color scheme.

Cultural Information

Light: Light shade is ideal. Takes full sun in areas that are warm in the winter, like south Florida or southern California.

Season: Spring through fall for most warmer areas. This plant mix takes temperatures from about 45 degrees to the low-90's. In a bit more shade, it withstands temperatures into the mid-90's. The leaves of the *Syngonium* show brown splotches in temperatures under 45 degrees.

Lifespan: Three to five months in this container.

Care: Fertilize on planting day with the slow-release mix described on page 26. Repeat if the leaves look yellowish or washed-out, although the fertilizer should last from six to nine months. Pinch the coleus to keep it full. I pinched this one about once a month.

Water: Water when the plants show signs of wilt or the soil feels dry when you push your fingertip up to your second knuckle into the potting mix. I watered this one every day (after it was about a month old) in mid summer and every other day in cooler weather.

Troubleshooting: No problems. This was a wonderful, trouble-free basket.

Quantity of Plants: Quantities for this pot size are given on the plant photos (opposite page). See pages 12, 14, and 15 for quantities needed for other container sizes and shapes.

Planting Plan: Easy. Alternate the *Syngonium* and coleus on both side layers as well as along the edge layers. Plant the New Guinea impatiens in the center. (*For full planting demo, see page 22.*)

For product sources, see page 15.

Syngonium 'Neon'
(6 plants from 4.5" pots)
Plant Profile: Page 155

Coleus 'Kingford Torch'
(6 plants from 4.5" pots)
Plant Profile: Page 140

**New Guinea Impatiens
'Infinity Salmon'**
(2 plants from 6" pots)
Plant Profile: Page 143

Long, Easy Trailer

20" double basic basket

Vinca vine is one of my favorite trailers because it quickly grows long without smothering surrounding plants. This arrangement was first used as a hanging basket (shown, opposite). After the vinca vine touched the ground, I moved it to a 48" column and gave it a hair cut!

Planting Sequence

Step 1: For the bottom side layer, alternate the vinca vine with the torenia.

Steps 2 & 3: Alternate the white begonias, torenia, and vinca vine in the top side layer. Plant the pink begonia in the center.

Step 4: Alternate the white begonias, torenia, and vinca vine around the edge. Be sure to put different plants above each other. (*For full planting demo, see pages 20-21.*)

Cultural Information

Light: Full sun to medium shade. Since wax begonias are sold for sun or shade, be sure to choose those that fit your light situation. Most take sun until the temperatures hit the low 90's. The red-leafed varieties take sun at higher temperatures, along with some of the newer, green-leafed types that should be labeled as sun begonias. Dragon wing begonias take full sun until the temperatures remain consistently higher than 94 degrees.

Season: Spring through fall for most areas. Also thrives in winter in areas where the temperatures stay above 33 degrees. This plant mix takes temperatures from about 38 degrees to the low 90's in full sun. In light shade, it withstands higher temperatures into the high 90's.

Lifespan: Four to five months in this container.

Care: Fertilize on planting day with the slow-release mix described on page 26. Repeat if the leaves look yellowish or washed-out, although the fertilizer should last from six to nine months. Trim the vinca vine if it gets too long.

Water: Water when the plants show signs of wilt or the soil feels dry when you push your fingertip up to your second knuckle into the potting mix. I watered this one every day in mid summer and every other day in cooler weather.

Troubleshooting: I planted the torenia as small seedlings while the other side plants were full, 4" specimen. Because of this size difference, the torenia was swallowed up by the other, larger plants. It is best to use plants that are the same size on planting day.

Quantity of Plants: Quantities for this pot size are given on the plant photos (opposite page). See page 12, 14, and 15 for quantities needed for other container sizes and shapes.

Planting Plan: See "Planting Sequence," left .

For product sources, see page 15.

Dragon Wing Begonia
(1 plant from a 3-gallon pot)
Plant profile: Page 138

Vinca Vine
(13 plants from 4" pots)
Plant profile: Page 155

Wax Begonia
(9 plants from 4" pots)
Plant profile: Page 132

'Catalina Blue' Torenia
(13 plants from 4" pots)
Plant profile: Page 152

Shades of Purple

16" single basic basket

This arrangement is a great example of impact from smaller containers. The 16" single basket grew into a giant masterpiece measuring over three feet across (see page 16)! And, the purple and lime green color scheme is a favorite of many visitors to our trial gardens.

The purples in this basket have red hues, whereas the purples in the companion basket below have blue hues.

Blue salvia and white begonias are planted underneath.

Companion basket. See page 119 to see it as a part of a group of three.

Cultural Information

Light: Light to medium shade in most areas. Takes full sun in areas that are warm in the winter, like south Florida or southern California.

Season: Spring through fall for most areas. Also thrives in winter in areas where the temperatures stay above 38 degrees. This plant mix takes temperatures from about 38 degrees to the low 90's in full sun. In light shade, it withstands higher temperatures into the high 90's.

Lifespan: Four to five months in this container.

Care: Fertilize on planting day with the slow-release mix described on page 26. Repeat if the leaves look yellowish or washed-out, although the fertilizer should last from six to nine months. Trim the torenia when it starts to droop. Pinch the coleus if it gets leggy. Keep all the edge plants shorter than the salvia in the middle. Salvia blooms more if you remove the dead flowers.

Water: Water when the plants show signs of wilt or the soil feels dry when you push your fingertip up to your second knuckle into the potting mix. I watered this one every day in mid summer (after it was about a month old) and every other day in cooler weather.

Troubleshooting: The torenia required two cutbacks which took a few weeks to recover from.

Quantity of Plants: Quantities for this pot size are given on the plant photos (opposite page). See pages 12, 14, and 15 for quantities needed for other container sizes and shapes.

Planting Plan: Alternate the impatiens, torenia, coleus, and creeping Jenny around the side layer. Repeat for the top side layer, putting different plants on top of one another. Plant the purple salvias as the centerpiece. *(For a full planting demo, see page 18-19.)*

For product sources, see page 15.

Salvia
(3 plants from 4" pots)
Plant profile: Page 150

'Dark Star' Coleus
(6 plants from 4" pots)
Plant profile: Page 140

Torenia
(6 plants from a 4" pots)
Plant profile: Page 153

Creeping Jenny
(6 plants from 4" pots)
Plant profile: Page 144

New Guinea Impatiens
(6 plants from 4" pots)
Plant profile: Page 143

Chapter 5

Layered Designs

Centerpiece

Edge Plants

Side Plants

1

2

3

Characteristics of layered designs:

❀ While 1-2-3 and striped designs feature identical plants on the side and edge layers, layered designs have different plants on these levels, as these window baskets demonstrate.

Benefits of layered designs

❀ Even growth habit

❀ Easy to design and plant

❀ Great for window boxes.

❀ Since some plants do poorly when planted in the sides, changing the edge plants gives you freedom to use those plants successfully. See pages 106-107 and 110-111 for examples.

Planting sequence at left:

Step 1: New Guinea impatiens and creeping Jenny are alternated in the side layer.

Step 2: Two *Juncus* plants are placed in the center.

Step 3: Coleus and creeping Jenny are alternated along the edge layer, which is different from the side layer shown in Step 1.

Above: A companion window box.

One of our Easiest!

16" single basic basket

This beautiful basket was one of the easiest to maintain in our trials. Although impatiens require more water than most other plants, we kept the basket under oak trees. Since plants require much less water in shade, we only watered it every day in the hottest part of the Georgia summer. It required no pinching at all, meaning we didn't touch it for its four month lifespan (other than watering).

I love the combination of jewel-toned purples and reds with stark white. The tailored look works well in both formal and informal gardens.

The flowers you plant under your baskets on columns make a difference to the overall look. The basket shown on the opposite page looks quite formal placed over tailored wax begonias. The same basket shown above looks less formal when placed over less-structured salvia.

Heights of the columns are also important. Size your column based on what you plan to plant underneath it, and whether you will include trailing plants in your basket. The column shown above is only 24 inches tall, which is too short for most gardens. The column opposite is 42 inches tall - much more appropriate for most underplantings.

See pages 118-121 for more about column heights.

Cultural Information

Light: Medium shade to full sun in cooler weather. Impatiens take sun in hot weather but don't like it. They also will drive you crazy with water needs in too much sun and heat, or with longer days in northeastern locations like New Hampshire. Most take sun until the temperatures hit the low 90's. If it's hotter than that, or summer days are quite long where you live, keep them in the shade.

Season: Spring through fall for most areas. Also thrives in winter in areas where the temperatures stay above 33 degrees. In light shade, it withstands higher temperatures into the high 90's.

Lifespan: Three to five months in this container. Lives longer in cooler weather, although it lasted four months for me in a hot Georgia summer!

Care: Fertilize on planting day with the slow-release mix described on page 26. Repeat if the leaves look yellowish or washed-out, although the fertilizer should last from six to nine months. The impatiens and begonias require no pinching. Persian shield may require pinching back if it gets leggy.

Water: Water when the plants show signs of wilt or the soil feels dry when you push your fingertip up to your second knuckle into the potting mix. I watered this one every day in mid summer (after it was about a month old) and every other day in cooler weather.

Troubleshooting: No problems with this arrangement.

Quantity of Plants: Quantities for this pot size are given on the plant photos (opposite page). See pages 12, 14, and 15 for quantities needed for other container sizes and shapes.

Planting Plan: Alternate red and violet impatiens around the side layer. Plant the Persian shield in the center. Surround it with white begonias planted around the edge. *(For full planting demo, see pages 18-19.)*

For product sources, see page 15.

Persian Shield
(1 plant from a 1-gallon pot)
Plant profile: Page 149

Wax Begonia
(12 plants from 4" pots)
Plant profile: Page 138

Red Impatiens
(6 plants from 4" pots)
Plant profile: Page 142

Violet Impatiens
(6 plants from 4" pots)
Plant profile: Page 142

Winter!

I didn't expect to like this arrangement when I planted it, but I couldn't resist trying these glamourous cabbages in the side of a basket. I thought they would get too big and hide the pansies planted along the top edge.

Was I ever wrong! The cabbages love being planted in the sides, and grew quite politely, leaving the pansies lots of space.

They call the purple one 'Dynasty Red.' I don't know why, when it looks more purple than red. Regardless, it looks terrific alternated with the 'Dynasty White' flowering cabbage.

And talk about easy! I very seldom had to do anything to this basket - not even water it! Imagine having this gorgeous arrangement outside all winter (or at least until the temperatures drop below 25 degrees) - and doing very little to keep it alive!

Cultural Information

Light: Light shade to full sun.

Season: Winter in most areas. These cabbages took temperatures down to the mid-20's. The pansies took a bit more cold.

Lifespan: Five to six months in this container.

Care: Fertilize on planting day with the slow-release mix described on page 26. Repeat if the leaves look yellowish or washed-out, although the fertilizer should last from six to nine months.

Water: Water when the plants show signs of wilt or the soil feels dry when you push your fingertip up to your second knuckle into the potting mix. You shouldn't need to water much in the cool weather if you have occasional rains. But watch closely because if you water too much, it might die. Conversely, very cold weather dries it out, so be sure it's watered before a real cold spell arrives.

Troubleshooting: The pansies went through periods of looking scraggly after really cold weather. They recovered quickly when the temperatures went up.

Quantity of Plants: Quantities for this pot size are given on the plant photos (opposite page). See pages 12, 14, and 15 for quantities needed for other container sizes and shapes.

Planting Plan: Easy. Alternate the two colors of cabbages for both side layers. Plant the *Juncus* grass in the center. Surround it with pansies. *(For full planting demo, see pages 20-21.)*

For product sources, see page 15.

Juncus Grass
(1 plant from a 1-gallon pot)
Plant Profile: Page 145

'Dynasty Red' Flowering Cabbage
(10 plants from 4.5" pots)
Plant Profile: Page 148

'Dynasty White' Flowering Cabbage
(11 plants from 4.5" pots)
Plant Profile: Page 148

Pansies
(14 plants from 4.5" pots)
Plant Profile: Page 148

Pastels

16" Imperial Planter

Alyssum is one of my favorite container plants, but it is too small to make a good centerpiece and doesn't like being planted in the sides. So, that leaves the top edge, where it finds the perfect home in this arrangement. Alyssum surrounds a double centerpiece of salvia and geraniums. Impatiens fill both side layers. I tried a few dusty millers in the sides, which you can still see. They didn't do well. However, the impatiens filled in the gaps nicely.

Alyssum is a valuable plant for containers because its texture is much different from most other plants. It is a great companion for geraniums, because their flowers are so much larger.

This basket was grown in the winter in Florida. It would work in most of the world when the temperatures are between 35 degrees and 85 degrees. The mix does not do well in hot weather because the alyssum prefers cooler temperatures.

The salvia and geranium centepieces did quite well together. Once again, a variety of flower shapes makes an interesting arrangement.

A companion basket with similar flower colors.

Cultural Information

Light: Light shade to full sun is ideal in the cooler temperatures required by the alyssum. However, if your summer is cool, and your days long, keep it in light shade because the impatiens will do better.

Season: Varied, based on where you live. Plant this mix when your temperatures range from 35 degrees to about 85 degrees. because the alyssum prefers cool weather.

Lifespan: Four to five months in this container.

Care: Fertilize on planting day with the slow-release mix described on page 26. Repeat if the leaves look yellowish or washed-out, although the fertilizer should last from six to nine months. Pinch the dead flowers off the geraniums. If the weather is particularly warm, you might have to trim the impatiens to keep them compact.

Water: Water when the plants show signs of wilt or the soil feels dry when you push your fingertip up to your second knuckle into the potting mix. I watered this one every three days because the weather was cool and the basket was in light shade.

Troubleshooting: No problems. This was a wonderful, trouble-free basket.

Quantity of Plants: Quantities for this pot size are given on the plant photos (opposite page). See pages 12, 14, and 15 for quantities needed for other container sizes and shapes.

Planting Plan: Alternate the two colors of impatiens to fill both side layers. Plant the geraniums and salvia close together in the center. Plant the alyssum around the top edge. (*For full planting demo, see pages 20-21.*)

For product sources, see page 15.

Geranium
(2 plants from 6" pots)
Plant Profile: Page 141

Blue Salvia
(2 plants from 6" pots)
Plant Profile: Page 150

Alyssum
(12 plants from 4.5" pots)
Plant Profile: Page 154

Salmon Impatiens
(9 plants from 4.5" pots)
Plant Profile: Page 142

White Impatiens
(9 plants from 4.5" pots)
Plant Profile: Page 142

Easy and Neat

16" single basic basket

This basket is one of the easiest we planted because it required almost no care other than watering. No trimming, pruning, or grooming. The layered look with these compact plants is naturally neat. And the New Guinea impatiens took a lot of heat, which surprised me.

Caladiums are excellent centerpiece plants because the large leaves contrast well with smaller leaves typical of most side and edge plantings.

Wax begonias and New Guinea impatiens are excellent choices for people who prefer a manicured look.

This arrangement is neat as long as you are judging it based on its growth habit as opposed to the amount of flower droppings. Impatiens drop a good bit, but I use them anyway over patios and decks. I wash the droppings away when I water the baskets.

A companion basket with the side and edge plants reversed.

Cultural Information

Light: Light to medium shade.

Season: Spring through fall for most warmer areas. This plant mix takes temperatures from about 62 degrees to the mid 90's. The caladiums don't do well in temperatures below 62 degrees.

Lifespan: Three to five months in this container.

Care: Fertilize on planting day with the slow-release mix described on page 26. Repeat if the leaves look yellowish or washed-out, although the fertilizer should last from six to nine months. That's it! This is one of the easiest combinations we grew.

Water: Water when the plants show signs of wilt or the soil feels dry when you push your fingertip up to your second knuckle into the potting mix. I watered this one every day (after it was about a month old) in mid summer.

Troubleshooting: The New Guinea impatiens were slow to start blooming, but once they flowered, they did really well. Japanese beetles attacked in early summer, and had to be sprayed.

Quantity of Plants: Quantities for this pot size are given on the plant photos (opposite page). See pages 12, 14, and 15 for quantities needed for other container sizes and shapes.

Planting Plan: Easy. Plant the impatiens in the side layer, followed by the caladium in the center. Plant the begonias around the top edge (*For full planting demo, see pages 18-19.*)

For product sources, see page 15.

Caladium
(1 plant from a 6" pot)
Plant Profile: Page 139

**New Guinea Impatiens
'Infinity Cherry Red'**
(8 plants from 4.5" pots)
Plant Profile: Page 143

Wax Begonia
(8 plants from 4.5" pots)
Plant Profile: Page 138

Blue, Pink, and Silver

16" single basic basket

Classic colors make up this arrangement, which is a great one for those who love pastels. This gave me a chance to use dusty miller, which doesn't like life in the sides of these containers. So, I tucked a few in along the top edge, and they loved it there!

This basket grew huge in diameter. So big, in fact, that we had to dig up the columns and put them farther apart! They started out being three feet apart, and the baskets grew together. So we redid them, this time four feet apart! See pages 122-123 for more about spacing columns.

This basket (left, on a 36" column) coordinates well with the taller one (on a 48" column) shown to the right.

The baskets are underplanted with salvia, torenia, and pentas.

Cultural Information

Light: Full sun to light shade.

Season: Spring through fall for most areas. Also thrives in winter in areas where the temperatures stay above 33 degrees. This plant mix takes temperatures from about 33 degrees to the low 90's in full sun. In light shade, it withstands higher temperatures into the high 90's.

Lifespan: Three to five months in this container. Lives longer in cooler weather, although it lasted four months for me in a hot Georgia summer!

Care: Fertilize on planting day with the slow-release mix described on page 26. Repeat if the leaves look yellowish or washed-out, although the fertilizer should last from six to nine months. Trim the torenia and the blue salvia back if either starts to droop.

Water: Water when the plants show signs of wilt or the soil feels dry when you push your fingertip up to your second knuckle into the potting mix. I watered this one every day (after it was about a month old) in mid summer.

Troubleshooting: The torenia required a hard cutback twice during this arrangement's lifespan. It needed about 2 weeks to recover from each cutback. Also, the blue salvia started to fall down the sides when the basket was mature. I should have planted the salvia in the center and the shorter pentas on the edge.

Quantity of Plants: Quantities for this size pot are given on the plant photos (opposite page). See pages 12, 14, and 15 for quantities needed for other container sizes and shapes.

Planting Plan: Alternate begonias and torenia around the side layer. Plant the penta in the center. Surround the penta with the dusty miller and blue salvia. *(For full planting demo, see pages 18-19.)*

For product sources, see page 15.

Dusty Miller
(plants from 4" pots)
Plant profile: Page 154

Blue Salvia
(4 plants from 4" pots)
Plant profile: Page 150

Penta
(1 plant from a 1-gallon pot)
Plant profile: Page 149

Torenia, Upright
(6 plants from 4" pots)
Plant profile: Page 153

White and Pink Begonias
(3 of each from 4" pots)
Plant profile: Page 138

Designed to Test

This basket is unusual for me because the sides are completely different from the top. Normally, I use the same mix on both, other than the centerpiece. But this time, I wanted to test the lovely *Schizanthus* 'Treasure Trove Bicolor.' Since many of my tests fail, I decided to plant it in the top because that is the easiest location to replace plants in case it died. I alternated it with yellow violas because I liked the combination of purple and yellow.

The sides of the basket were planted with tried-and-true impatiens and *Lysimachia* 'Outback Sunset.'

The label on the Schizanthus (also called poor man's orchid) stated that it was short lived, and that was the case. It flowered for about a month, and I replaced it with some impatiens when it stopped flowering.

Companion baskets with similar colors.

Cultural Information

Light: Light shade to full sun is ideal in areas where the temperatures are fairly cool (38 to 85 degrees) and the days short. This is not a good choice for hot (over 85 degrees) sun, or areas where the days are long in summer, like New Hampshire. Stick to light shade in these places or the impatiens will need too much water.

Season: Needs cool temperatures for the *Schizanthus* and the violas. Ideal for this mix is 38 to 85 degrees.

Lifespan: Four to five months in this container.

Care: Fertilize on planting day with the slow-release mix described on page 26. Repeat if the leaves look yellowish or washed-out, although the fertilizer should last from six to nine months.

Water: Water when the plants show signs of wilt or the soil feels dry when you push your fingertip up to your second knuckle into the potting mix. I watered this one every three days (after it was about a month old). As the basket grew, I watered every other day. (Remember, this is a cool weather basket! The impatiens would definitely need daily watering in the sun in warmer temperatures.)

Troubleshooting: I replaced the *Schizanthus* after about two months, but I didn't mind because the plant label had said that it was short-lived. Other than that, this was an easy basket.

Quantity of Plants: Quantities for this pot size are given on the plant photos (opposite page). See pages 12, 14, and 15 for quantities needed for other container sizes and shapes.

Planting Plan: Alternate the impatiens and 'Outback Sunset' for both side layers. Plant the salvia in the top. Plant violas and *Schizanthus* along the top edge. (*For full planting demo, see pages 20-21.*)

For product sources, see page 15.

Salvia
(3 plants from 6" pots)
Plant Profile: Page 150

Violas
(8 plants from 4.5" pots)
Plant Profile: Page 153

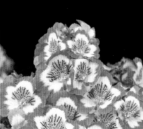
Schizanthus
'Treasure Trove Bicolor'
(2 plants from 1-gallon pots)
Plant Profile: Page 155

Lysimachia
'Outback Sunset'
(7 plants from 4.5" pots)
Plant Profile: Page 146

Lilac and Red Impatiens
(7 of each from 4.5" pots)
Plant Profile: Page 142

Delphiniums

16" Imperial Planter

I planted this basket to take advantage of some gorgeous delphiniums I found at a garden center. I knew they wouldn't bloom for the five months that I aim for, but I just couldn't resist them. The snapdragons planted on either side don't bloom continually, like the delphinium. By planting the two together, at least one of them bloomed the entire time this basket lived.

I wasn't thrilled with the proportions of the basket. I like centerpieces to be fatter. But the beauty of the flowers made up for this problem.

The sides of the basket are planted with some of the most dependable bloomers, begonias. The variegated mint added leaf color.

Snapdragons have not done well for me when planted in the sides of these baskets. They do quite well planted on the top, provided you are prepared for them to go out of bloom sometimes.

Cultural Information

Light: Light shade to full sun is ideal.

Season: Varies, based on where you live. Plant this mix when your temperatures range from 33 degrees to about 80 degrees.

Lifespan: Four to five months in this container, but only if you replace the delphinium after about two months.

Care: Fertilize on planting day with the slow-release mix described on page 26. Repeat if the leaves look yellowish or washed-out, although the fertilizer should last from six to nine months. Pinch the mint as needed to keep it even and full. It will trail if you leave it alone, and you may prefer it that way.

Water: Water when the plants show signs of wilt or the soil feels dry when you push your fingertip up to your second knuckle into the potting mix. I watered this one every three days (after it was about a month old).

Troubleshooting: No problems. This was a wonderful, trouble-free basket.

Quantity of Plants: Quantities for this pot size are given on the plant photos (opposite page). See pages 12, 14, and 15 for quantities needed for other container sizes and shapes.

Planting Plan: A bit complicated. Alternate the two colors of begonias and the variegated mint around the two side layers. Plant the delphinium in the middle. Plant three snapdragons on one side of the delphinium and three on the other. Fill in with white begonias. *(For full planting demo, see page 20-21.)*

This basket hung next to the one shown at right in our trial gardens.

For product sources, see page 15.

Delphinium
(plant from a 1-gallon pot)
Plant Profile: Page 154

Pink Wax Begonia
(6 plants from 4.5" pots)
Plant Profile: Page 138

White Wax Begonia
(10 plants from 4.5" pots)
Plant Profile: Page 138

**Plectranthus Variegata
or Variegated Mint**
(6 plants from 4.5" pots)
Plant Profile: Page 147

Snapdragons
(6 plants from 4.5" pots)
Plant Profile: Page 155

Chapter 6

Baskets on Columns
In the Garden

After

Before

When I first began my trials with side-planted hanging baskets, I quickly ran out of space to hang them. So, I began putting them on columns in the garden.

Containers are best seen at eye level. Details of the flowers are easier to see, and the visual impact is increased.

Many of today's gardens are small. The best way to use space in a small garden is to go vertical. Baskets on columns do this well.

Maintaining your containers is much easier if you don't have to bend down. I have really enjoyed grooming my baskets on columns, partly because it is so physically easy.

And talk about impact! A group of three baskets on columns in your front yard is traffic-stopping gorgeous!

Included in this chapter:

❀ Choosing the right column height

❀ Spacing the columns

❀ Coordinating the flowers planted underneath

Above and left: My walkway during summer trials.

Choosing Column Height

Column height depends on the types of plants in your baskets. Baskets with trailing plants do best on 36", 42", and 48" columns. Baskets with mounding plants can go as low as 24" columns if you are planting short plants underneath.

Above: These baskets on columns planted with mounding plants are 24", 30", and 36" tall. That is the shortest I would ever use for these columns. Mixed salvia is planted in the ground. The yellow flowers in the background are melampodium. See pages 50-51 for a profile of the container on the shortest column.

Right: These baskets on columns planted with trailing plants are 36", 42", and 48" tall. I like this size range best for groups of three columns. White wax begonias are planted in the ground below. See pages 98-99 for a profile of the front container.

For container sources, go to www.sideplanting.com

Choosing Column Height

If your basket grouping includes both mounding and trailing plants, stick to columns measuring at least 36" tall. This grouping, photographed from both sides, features columns of 36", 42", and 48".

This is the largest grouping I have ever done, totalling six columns.

Above: Notice how the plants in the containers are different but stick to the same color scheme of lime, red, and purple. The flowers planted in the ground repeat the color theme. They include red and blue salvia, yellow marigolds, hot pink periwinkles, and 'Gold Mound' duranta.

Right: The front basket is a 14" single. The middle row are 16" singles. The center basket in the back (tallest) row is a 20" double, with a 16" double on each side.

I placed the baskets with trailing plants on the largest 48" columns. Although the sweet potato vines trail well on these tall columns, they tend to take over the other plants in the baskets. Some signs of coleus that are almost smothered by the vines are shown in the baskets on the tallest columns.

For container sources, go to www.sideplanting.com

Spacing the Columns

The goal of spacing your columns is to keep the plants in the different baskets from touching one another when they are mature. That can be deceiving in the beginning because the baskets grow so large as they mature. I started with a 30" distance between columns, and they grew together quickly. I now use a minimum of 40" in between the columns in a single grouping.

It is better to put too much space between the baskets than not enough. I had to move six columns one summer because the baskets they supported grew together. Once you have done that once, you'll never do it again! The baskets pictured on these two pages are a full 5' apart.

For container sources, go to www.sideplanting.com

Coordinate the Garden

Plants under your baskets don't need to be an exact match to the plants in the baskets, but they need to coordinate. I first planted rust coleus under these pastel baskets and it looked awful! I replaced them with the salvia, pentas, and torenia you see here. This plant group, along with the plants in the baskets, took the summer heat really well.

These baskets are a full 4' apart. The posts measure 36", 42", and 48" high.

Above: The left basket is a 16" double (profile on page 53); the center, a 16" single (profile, page 111), while the basket to the right is a 20" double.

For container sources, go to www.sideplanting.com

More Design Ideas For the Garden

After

Before

When I first began working on container garden books, I was concerned that it would be quite difficult to get real impact with containers in the garden. Have I ever learned a lot since then!

Great containers transform gardens. I first learned this when I began putting these large containers on columns. Although the garden had a lot going for it other than the columns, it looked non-descript when the columns weren't there.

I also learned the impact of containers in my own home, shown at left. I had these containers out in spring, summer, and fall. Every new visitor to my home raved about how gorgeous my home looked.

In winter, I removed the containers. Although the house looked exactly the same, the comments stopped coming!

Granted, since I am a gardening fanatic, I may take it a bit over the top at my own home. But simple fixes, as shown in this chapter, can also have major impact on the appearance of homes of people who are not so fanatical!

Hanging baskets, window boxes, and baskets on columns - along with annual plantings in the ground - completely transformed my porch.

Window boxes are ideal for railings. These are planted with dracaena 'Lemon Lime' as centerpieces and impatiens, creeping Jenny, and coleus as side and edge plantings.

The basket on a column next to the steps is planted with a caladium centerpiece along with begonias and New Guinea impatiens along the edge and in the sides.

Look at the photo to the left. See the three hooks installed in the top beam for hanging baskets? With 70 inches in between the columns, I planned for three baskets of staggered heights. But, they quickly grew together. One basket - and only a small one (16" single layer) filled that large space! I am continually surprised by how large plants grow in these containers!

Before

For container sources, see page 15.

After

Easy Transformation...

Before

After

For container sources, see page 15.

What a difference a day makes! That's all the time it took to plant this basket on a column, two window boxes, and the annuals below in the garden.

The window boxes are actually different sizes! One is 30" wide and the other is 36" wide. I used what I had on hand and, luckily, they worked out well.

Right: Another view of the windows that shows the 'Kong' coleus, melampodium, and red begonias planted in the garden.

Below: Purple petunias and mixed salvia are planted across the walk.

Deck Transformation

Before

The simple addition of three wall pots completely transformed my deck. I chose two different sizes. The large one is a 20" double and the other two are 16" singles.

They looked good the day they were planted. The change you see from the photo below to the photo to the right is typical of these containers. They change as they fill out and grow.

Just Planted

This grouping is just one more lesson on how large the plants in these containers grow - especially in long, warm, growing seasons. Although the spacing of the containers looks perfect on planting day (near right), they could have used some more space two months later (far right)! The grouping turned into a wall of flowers. You can't tell where one pot begins and the other ends.

Wall pot, upper left: Profile on pages 58-59.

Lower left: Profile on pages 48-49.

For container sources, see page 15.

After, two months later

Arbors

I designed this arbor to accommodate a seating area as well as lots of containers. It works great, holding hundreds of colorful flowers just as I wanted. The mulch floor is ideal for flowers because they can shed their little hearts out without making a mess.

Hanging baskets are hung from the beams, while wall pots are hung from the back wall.

Measuring only eight by ten feet, this arbor is ideal for someone who wants a lot of flowers in a small space. It was constructed by my friend, Tim Hadsell, of Greenacres, Florida.

The red flowers in the front are geraniums, planted next to yellow melampodium and pink cleomes. The pots feature a mass of colorful flowers and leaves, including pentas, daisies, coleus, cosmos, dragon wing begonias, petunias, variegated mint, melampodium, double impatiens.

For container sources, see page 15.

Chapter 8

Best Plants for Instant Containers

Lilac Impatiens
Plant Profile: Page 142

Coleus 'Wizard Golden'
Plant Profile: Page 140

Mammey Croton
Plant Profile: Page 154

'Odorata' Begonia

Salvia
Plant Profile: Page 150

This chapter gives you plant profiles of the top 36 plants we tested, along with shorter descriptions of another 23 plants that deserve mention. But don't limit yourself to only these plants because instant container gardening gives you the opportunity to really have fun experimenting with new varieties. Let us know how you do at info@easygardencolor.com!

We classify plants as low, medium, or high with both salt and wind tolerance. Here are definitions of these terms:

<u>Salt Tolerance:</u> *Low* refers to plants that do not tolerate salt spray on their leaves. *Medium* refers to plants that take some salt on their leaves. *High* refers to plants that take direct oceanfront conditions, provided they are somewhat back from the shoreline.

<u>Wind Tolerance:</u> *Low* refers to plants that like fairly protected locations. *Medium* refers to plants that take winds produced in more open locations but not extreme sites, like oceanfront or in a wind tunnel created by buildings. *High* refers to plants that are the most wind-tolerant available. In storms where winds reach 30 to 40 miles per hour for more than a few hours, even plants with high-wind tolerance suffer leaf burn. However, the plants with high-wind tolerance obviously sustain less damage than the ones with low-wind tolerance. The leaf burn does not heal. New leaves grow and eventually replace the ones that are damaged. None of the plants in this book can sustain severe tropical storm or hurricane-force winds without damage.

Above: A "leftover" basket mounted on a post. Read more about "leftover" baskets on page 45.

Left: We test plants grown in the ground as well as in containers. The success rate for plants in containers is much higher. Also, notice how well the baskets on posts coordinate with the garden underneath.

Plant Profiles: The High Performers

Begonia, Dragon Wing *(Begonia 'Dragon Wing')*

Characteristics and Care

Use: Mounding or centerpiece plant. One of the best for the sides of a hanging basket.
Growth rate: Medium.
Size: **In the top of a large container, grows 2' tall by 1' wide. Smaller if planted in the side of a basket, about 8" tall.**
Colors: Red or pink.
Average life: 6 months.
Cautions: None known.
Care: Very easy. Fertilize on planting day with the slow-release mix described on page 26. Repeat if the leaves look yellowish or washed-out, although the fertilizer should last from 6 to 9 months. Trim off the tips if the plants become too large.

Dragon wing begonias are one of the highest performers in our trials, blooming continually with an impressive percentage of color for at least six months. Although they grow much taller than the more common wax begonias, I prefer them in the sides and along the edges of instant containers.

Companions: Use the reds with bright colors. Or, combine them with golden shrimp plants and Persian shield for shade drama. Mix the pink with more subdued yellows and blues.

Growing Conditions

Season: Any frost-free season.
Light: Medium shade to full sun. Needs some break from sun if temperatures stay consistently about 94 degrees.
Water: Medium.
Salt tolerance: Medium.
Wind tolerance: Low.
Zone: Use as an annual. Tolerant of light frost but not a freeze.
Pest problems: Occasional fungus, caterpillars, or snails.

Begonia, Wax *(Begonia x semper. Cultorum)*

Characteristics and Care

Use: Mounding plant.
Growth rate: Medium.
Size: **In the top of a container, grows about 8" tall by 5" wide. Smaller if planted in the side of a basket, about 4" to 6" tall.**
Colors: Red, pink, or white flowers on green or bronze leaves.
Average life: 4 to 6 months.
Cautions: None known.
Care: Very easy. Fertilize on planting day with the slow-release mix described on page 26. The fertilizer should last from 6 to 9 months.

Wax begonias are one of the most commonly used annuals in the world because of their toughness and dependability. They are not as dramatic as dragon wing or gumdrop begonias but work well in the sides of hanging baskets. I find the white-flowered wax begonia with green leaves particularly useful.

Companions: Contrast these small flowers with larger ones, like geraniums and petunias. For a beautiful hanging basket, plant hot pink geraniums in the top. Then alternate white begonias and midnight blue petunias along the rim of the basket, as well as on the sides.

Growing Conditions

Season: Any frost-free season. Prefers temperatures below the high-90's.
Light: Medium shade to full sun in the cooler areas, but some burn in the summer sun. Bronze-leafed varieties, as well as new, sun-tolerant green ones, are more sun-tolerant in the heat.
Water: Medium.
Salt tolerance: Medium.
Wind tolerance: Medium.
Zone: Use as an annual. Tolerant of light frost but not a freeze.
Pest problems: Occasional fungus, shown by leaf spots.

Bromeliad *(many different genuses and species)*

Characteristics and Care

Use: Centerpiece or accent.
Growth rate: Slow.
Size: Varies greatly by species, from tiny to over 5' tall.
Colors: All!
Average life: Single plant lives about 2 years but sends up babies to replace itself.
Cautions: Serrated leaves on some varieties can be quite hazardous.
Care: Fertilize on planting day with the slow-release mix described on page 26. Avoid getting fertilizer in the center of the plants.

Bromeliads are one of the highest performers in our trials. Over 2500 different types of bromeliads have been identified, varying greatly in size and color. Some have gorgeous flowers that bloom for two to four months at a time. They are quite happy in the same pot for years on end.
Trimming: The mother plant dies after flowering and producing pups (babies). Trim off the dead plant after it becomes brown. Leave the remaining pups to grow where they are or separate them to plant in other pots. Since this only has to be done every few years, this is truly an easy plant.

Growing Conditions

Season: All year. Bring inside if frost threatens.
Light: Medium to light shade. Takes more light in winter. If used inside, will continue to bloom in deep shade until that flower dies.
Water: Low, but tolerates daily watering if planted with impatiens.
Salt tolerance: High for thick-leafed varieties.
Wind tolerance: High for thick-leafed varieties.
Zone: 9b to 11. Protect from freezes.
Pest problems: None serious.

Caladium *(Caladium x hortulanum)*

Characteristics and Care

Use: Mounding plant or centerpiece.
Growth rate: Medium
Size: 6" to 30" tall, depending on variety.
Colors: Shades of white, green, red, and pink.
Average life: Normally used for just one summer.
Cautions: Poisonous.
Care: Fertilize on planting day with the slow-release mix described on page 26. If you feel really energetic, removing the nondescript flowers increases leaf production.

Caladiums are one of the highest performers for summer color. I used them extensively as centerpieces. Be sure you know what the mature size is of the ones you buy. The newer dwarf varieties are not tall enough for centerpiece positions.
Companions: Mix them with flowering plants in colors that coordinate with the leaves. I frequently use them with begonias, torenia, and coleus.

Growing Conditions

Season: Summer.
Light: Medium shade to full sun, depending on type.
Water: Medium.
Salt tolerance: Medium.
Wind tolerance: Low.
Zone: Grown throughout the world as a summer annual.
Pest Problems: Slugs or snails.

Plant Profiles: The High Performers

Coleus *(Solenostemon scutellarioides)*

Characteristics and Care

Use: Smaller types for mounding plants and larger ones for center-pieces.
Growth rate: Medium.
Size: Varies greatly by variety, 6" to 36" tall and equally as wide.
Colors: Shades of red, white, yellow, and green and purple.
Average life: 6 months.
Cautions: None known
Care: Fertilize on planting day with the slow-release mix described on page 26. Pinch the tips monthly if plant becomes too large. If you delay this trimming, it may take them a while to look good again.

'Gay's Delight' 'Dark Star'
'Defiance' 'Crime Scene'

Growing Conditions

Season: Any time temperatures remain over 38 degrees.
Light: Prefers some shade, but many of the newer varieties take full sun.
Water: High.
Salt tolerance: Medium.
Wind tolerance: Medium.
Zone: Use as an annual.
Pest problems: Occasional aphids, mites, mealybugs, slugs, and snails.

Coleus are one of the highest performers in our trials, thriving as centerpieces or planted in the sides. New ones are constantly appearing, which makes identifying their mature size sometimes difficult at the garden center. But their leaves are so varied that we put up with this inconvenience. They produce some of the most beautiful leaf patterns in the world.
Companions: Coordinate coleus leaves with other leaf or flower colors. Try lime green with dark burgundy for a dramatic theme. Many combinations are shown throughout this book.

Daisy, California Bush *(Gamolepis chrysanthemoides)*

Characteristics and Care

Use: Centerpiece.
Growth rate: Medium.
Size: About 18" tall by 12" wide.
Colors: Yellow.
Average life: Looks good for about 6 months in the same container.
Cautions: None known.
Care: Very easy. Fertilize on planting day with the slow-release mix described on page 26. Blooms more if old blooms are removed.

Growing Conditions

Season: Prefers temperatures between 35 and 90 degrees.
Light: Full sun.
Water: Medium.
Salt tolerance: Medium.
Wind tolerance: Medium.
Zone: Although this plant is used as a perennial in other warm parts of the world, it performs best as an annual in most areas. Protect from frost.
Pest problems: Spider mites occasionally. I have never had a pest on this plant in my gardens.

California bush daisy (yellow flower, above) is one of the highest performing daisies from our trials. The flowers are not as large as the cape or marguerite daisies, but the plant lasts longer than they do. It blooms almost continuously. The plant also performs well in the ground, but don't expect more than about six months' use.
Companions: Since California daisies look great with reds and blues, the above mixed arrangement is ideal. Also, try it with other shapes and sizes of flowers, like salvias, geraniums, and pentas.

Dracaena 'Lemon Lime' *(Dracaena deremensis 'Lemon-Lime)*

Characteristics and Care

Use: Centerpiece.
Growth rate: Medium.
Size: Use small ones in instant containers, up to 24" tall.
Colors: Leaves are striped with different shades of green.
Average life: 10 to 15 years if moved inside when freezes threaten.
Cautions: None known.
Care: Very easy. Fertilize every 6 to 9 months with the slow-release mix described on page 26.

Dracaenas are one of the most common indoor plants. They work well outdoors as well, provided they are protected from frost. Most plants that grow in dense shade are dark green, so the 'Lemon Lime' dracaena is a welcome newcomer, with its unique leaf color. It is one of the few indoor plants that gives a significant amount of color and lasts for years on end.

Companions: In dense shade, use this plant as a centerpiece and surround it with pothos, crotons, or other small plants from the house plant section of the garden center.

Growing Conditions

Season: All year. Protect from frost.
Light: Light, medium, or dense shade.
Water: Medium.
Salt tolerance: Unknown.
Wind tolerance: Medium.
Zone: 10 to 11. Protect from freezes in cooler area if used outdoors.
Pest problems: Scales and mealybugs, particularly if used indoors or under screening.

Geranium, Upright *(Pelargonium x hortorum)*

Characteristics and Care

Use: Most commonly used as a centerpiece.
Growth rate: Medium.
Size: 12" to 14" tall.
Colors: Many shades of red, pink, peach, white, and lavender.
Average life: 5 to 6 months.
Cautions: None known.
Care: Fertilize on planting day with a slow-release mix. Geraniums look better with the dead flowers removed, which can be tedious. I sometimes let them go and am surprised at how well they do!

Geraniums: Geraniums do well in the warm, dry weather. They don't tolerate extreme heat well. They thrive in containers and are one of our best choices for centerpieces. Since they look better when dead headed (removing spent flowers), it is easier to use a few in an easy-to-reach pot than hundreds in the landscape.

Companions: I like them with flowers that have different shapes, like salvias and petunias. Geraniums, petunias, and alyssum are one of my favorite combinations.

Growing Conditions

Season: Prefer temperatures from 33 to 90 degrees. I keep them in light shade in higher temperatures, up to 95 degrees.
Light: Light shade to full sun.
Water: Medium.
Salt tolerance: Medium.
Wind tolerance: Medium.
Zone: Use as an annual. Tolerant of light frost but not a freeze.
Pest problems: Fungus.

Plant Profiles: The High Performers

Grass, Fountain *(Pennisetum spp.)*

Characteristics and Care

Use: Centerpiece.
Growth rate: Medium.
Size: **In the top of a container, grows about 3' by 2.5' wide.**
Colors: Green, bronze, gray.
Average life: 6 months.
Cautions: None known.
Care: Very easy. Fertilize on planting day with the slow-release mix described on page 26. The fertilizer should last from 6 to 9 months.

Growing Conditions

Season: Protect from frost.
Light: Light shade to full sun.
Water: Low.
Salt tolerance: Medium.
Wind tolerance: Medium.
Zone: 5 to 11.
Pest problems: None known in pots.

Fountain grass has a tall, graceful form. It looks get when not blooming, but better when the fuzzy seed fronds form. They last a month or so. And, fountain grass is easy to care for - not much fertilizer, not much water, no trimming in pots. This is one of our best centerpiece plants.
Companions: While they look very dramatic alone in huge pots, I love grasses with flowers. It looks good with pentas, lantana and verbena. They also work well with leaf color, like coleus.

Impatiens *(Impatiens wallerana)*

Characteristics and Care

Use: Mounding plant that works well alone or mixed with other bright colors.
Growth rate: Fast.
Size: Generally, in containers, they get 12" by 12"
Colors: Red, salmon, orange, white, purple or pink.
Average life: 3 to 5 months.
Cautions: Very high water use.
Care: Fertilize on planting day with the slow-release mix described on page 26. Trim off the tips if leggy.

Growing Conditions

Season: Perform best in temperatures of 40 to 90 degrees, but grow in shade into the high 90's.
Light: Medium shade to full sun. Avoid sun in high temperatures or long, sunny days.
Water: High (as much as twice daily) in full sun, medium in shade.
Salt tolerance: Medium.
Wind tolerance: Low.
Zone: Use as annual. Very susceptible to frost.
Pest Problems: Fungus and slugs.

Impatiens: are the world's most popular annual plant. They literally bloom their heads off from the day you put them in till the day you take them out. And they thrive in the sides of instant containers. But be prepared to water them quite a bit!
Companions: Mix them with other annuals, particularly petunias, salvias, and begonias. Or combine bright colored impatiens with other bright colors in the light shade. The whites and pale pinks are best in medium shade or areas where you can view them at night.

Impatiens, Double *(Impatiens spp)*

Characteristics and Care

Use: Mounding plant.
Growth rate: Fast.
Size: Grows to 18" tall as a centerpiece.
Grows about 8" to 12" tall in the sides.
Colors: Red, pink, purple, orange, peach, and white.
Average life: 3 to 5 months.
Cautions: None known.
Care: Fertilize on planting day with the slow-release mix described on page 26. No deadheading required so there's no special care required other than frequent waterings.

Double impatiens are spectacular. They are one of the top ten container plants on the market today, providing all the advantages of the regular impatiens with prettier flowers. The flowers look like roses. They bloom non-stop, so you can count on them looking great all the time. About the only disadvantage is they do shed a lot in containers.
Companions: Be careful what you put around them because they are fairly aggressive growers. Try them with dark Persian shield, wax begonias and dragon wing begonias.

Growing Conditions

Season: Perform best in temperatures of 40 to 90 degrees, but grow in shade into the high 90's.
Light: Medium shade to full sun. Avoid sun in high temperatures or long, sunny days.
Water: Medium in shade and very high in sun - as much as twice a day.
Salt tolerance: Low.
Wind tolerance: Low.
Zone: Very sensitive to the lightest frost so bring them indoors.
Pest problems: Fungus and slugs.

Impatiens, New Guinea *(Impatiens x New Guinea Hybrids)*

Characteristics and Care

Use: Mounding plant that works well as a centerpiece or in the sides.
Growth rate: Medium.
Size: About 8" to 12" tall in the top of a container, smaller in the sides.
Colors: Iridescent pinks, oranges, reds, purples, peaches, whites, and multi-colored.
Average life: 4 to 6 months.
Cautions: None known.
Care: Fertilize on planting day with the slow-release mix described on page 26.

New Guinea impatiens have more color impact than any other plant you can use in a container. Both their flowers and leaves are colorful, with the most color coming from the flowers. They do extremely well in instant containers, even in the sides. These impatiens are very easy to grow, not requiring quite as much water as regular impatiens.
Companions: One great and easy idea is to use these at the base of bromeliads. Another dramatic combination is to use them as the centerpiece plant surrounded by the lime-green sweet potato and bright coleus.

Growing Conditions

Season: Perform best in temperatures of 40 to 90 degrees, but grow in shade into the high 90's.
Light: Medium shade to full sun. Avoid sun in high temperatures or long, sunny days.
Water: High, but not as much as regular impatiens.
Salt tolerance: Medium.
Wind tolerance: Medium.
Zone: Use as an annual. Very sensitive to the slightest frost.
Pest problems: Fungus and slugs.

Plant Profiles: The High Performers

Ivy *(Hedera helix)*

Characteristics and Care

Use: Trailing plant.
Growth rate: Slow.
Size: **Trails about 12" over the sides of a pot.**
Colors: Green or variegated.
Average life: Lives for many years.
Cautions: Green varieties are invasive in some areas.
Care: Fertilize every 6 to 9 months with the slow-release mix described on page 26. Trim off the tips if the plants become too large.

Ivy is one of the best trailing plants, especially because most garden centers stock it in small hanging baskets, with vines already 10"-12" long. Pull them apart (at the roots) into small sections and use them in the sides of your container for instant trailers.

Companions: Pair the ivy with almost any other plant - from flowers like impatiens to formal topiaries. Many new, variegated ivy plants are appearing on the market each season to supplement the traditional, dark green types.

Growing Conditions

Season: Varies with type. Some grow all year, while others die in very cold weather.
Light: Sun to dense shade in winter. Shade in summer.
Water: Low. Very adaptable to what is needed by the plants around it.
Salt tolerance: Low.
Wind tolerance: High.
Zone: Varies with type.
Pest problems: Scale and mold.

Jenny, Creeping or Lysimachia 'Goldilocks' *(Lysimachia mummularia)*

Characteristics and Care

Use: Trailing plant for the edges or sides.
Growth rate: Medium.
Size: **Trails over the edge of the pot to at least 18 inches, but it takes a while to get there!**
Colors: Lime green.
Average life: We kept them in pots up to 6 months. Grows as a perennial in much of the world.
Cautions: None known.
Care: Fertilize every 6 to 9 months with the slow-release mix described on page 26. Trim the tips as needed.

Creeping Jenny is one of the best trailing plants for instant containers. Most long trailers are either so fast-growing that they take over the whole pot, like the sweet potato vines, or so slow that the other plants in the pot are dead by the time they reach an acceptable size. Not so for Creeping Jenny. It is easy to grow - and quick to reach a good size without overwhelming the arrangement. It works well in striped or 1-2-3 arrangements.

Companions: This plant works beautifully in almost any style. It not only compliments cottage flowers but tropical arrangements as well.

Growing Conditions

Season: All year in frost-free areas.
Light: Medium shade to full sun. Burns a bit in constant sun in the hottest part of summer.
Water: Medium.
Salt tolerance: Unknown.
Wind tolerance: Medium.
Zone: Hardy to zone 3. Use as an annual in frost-free areas.
Pest problems: No pests bothered our Creeping Jenny. According to Euro American growers, watch for aphids and whiteflies. Foliage easily damaged by sprays.

Juncus, Rush *(Juncus effusus)*

Characteristics and Care

Use: Centerpiece.
Growth rate: Slow.
Size: 15" to 24" tall.
Colors: Green
Average life: Perennial to zone 4. Exact lifespan unknown.
Cautions: Unknown.
Care: Fertilize every 6 to 9 months with the slow-release mix described on page 26.

Growing Conditions

Season: Dies back somewhat in when the temperatures hit the low 20's. Best used in spring, summer, and fall.
Light: Sun to light shade.
Water: Low to high. Very adaptable to what is needed by the plants around it.
Salt tolerance: Unknown.
Wind tolerance: Unknown.
Zone: Hardy to zone 4.
Pest problems: Scale and mold.

Juncus is one of the best grasses for centerpieces. It's tall stature keeps it well above most plants used for edge plantings. It's long, straight form is quite different from many other grasses, making it an interesting focal point. And it is incredibly easy to grow!

Companions: This is a very versatile plant. Use it with mixed flowers for a cottage garden look, or structured begonias and impatiens for a more elegant look.

Lamium 'White Nancy' *(Lamium maculatum 'White Nancy')*

Characteristics and Care

Use: Trailing plant for edges or sides.
Growth rate: Medium.
Size: Trails about 8 inches down the side of a pot.
Colors: Green and white leaves with small, white flowers. Use this plant for its leaves.
Average life: Perennial. Lifespan unknown.
Cautions: Unknown.
Care: Fertilize every 6 to 9 months with the mix described on page 26. Trim off the tips if the plant become too large.

Growing Conditions

Season: For containers, spring, summer, and fall. Winter in frost-free areas.
Light: Medium shade to full sun in the cooler weather, but burns in the summer sun.
Water: Medium. We watered the pots shown every third day.
Salt tolerance: Unknown.
Wind tolerance: Unknown.
Zone: Hardy to zone 3.
Pest problems: Unknown.

Lamium is a favorite in northern gardens. We were thrilled with the results with the samples that Proven Winners sent us. As a trailing plant, it worked beautifully to define other plants like verbena and petunias. Lamium adds a distinct texture and feel to hanging baskets. We did not test it in the ground.

Companions: Use with other trailing plants like verbena and petunias. I particularly like this one with different shades of purple.

Plant Profiles: The High Performers

Lysimachia 'Outback Sunset' *(Lysimachia 'Outback Sunset')*

Characteristics and Care

Use: Trailing plant for sides or edges.
Growth rate: Medium.
Size: Grows about 8" down the sides of a pot.
Colors: Yellow and green leaves with yellow flowers.
Average life: 4 to 6 months.
Cautions: None known.
Care: Fertilize every 6 to 9 months with the mix described on page 26. Trim off the tips if the plants become too large.

Growing Conditions

Season: Any frost-free season.
Light: Medium shade to full sun in the cool season, but burns in the summer sun.
Water: Medium.
Salt tolerance: Unknown.
Wind tolerance: Unknown.
Zone: Hardy to zone 7a.
Pest problems: Unknown.

Lysimachia: I first tried a lysimachia 'Golden Globes' with solid green leaves, which had a very short bloom time. However, I was thrilled with the 'Outback Sunset' because the leaves give color all the time, even when the flowers are dormant. The bright color of the leaves is quite showy, and this plant is very easy to grow, performing extremely well in our trials.
Companions: Use it with plants that have dark flowers or leaves. It's dynamite with New Guinea impatiens, crotons, ti plants, and trailing torenia.

Melampodium *(Melampodium paludosum)*

Characteristics and Care

Use: Mounding plant for sides and edges.
Growth rate: Fast.
Size: About 12"tall.
Colors: Golden yellow.
Average life: 5 to 6 months.
Cautions: None known.
Care: Easy, except they like a lot of water, particularly in hot weather. Fertilize on planting day with the slow-release mix described on page 26. No trimming or deadheading required.

Growing Conditions

Season: Summer. It does not like temperatures lower than 50 degrees.
Light: Medium shade to full sun. Needs much less water in shade.
Water: Medium to high. In a pot, it can require daily watering when in sun.
Salt tolerance: Medium.
Wind tolerance: Medium.
Zone: Summer annual.
Pest problems: Occasional fungus.

Melampodium is one of my favorite yellow-flowering container plants. It blooms well all summer - one of the few annual plants that will. The daisy-like flowers add a mass of yellow to any arrangement.
Companions: An easy summer arrangement includes melampodium with red or hot pink pentas and trailing blue torenia.

Mint, Variegated *(Plectranthus coleoides 'Variegata')*

Characteristics and Care

Use: Trailing or mounding plant. Good for sides and edges.
Growth rate: Medium.
Size: Trails 36" over the edge of a pot.
Colors: Light green and white.
Average life: 6 months.
Cautions: None known.
Care: Very easy. Fertilize every 6 to 9 months with the slow-release mix described on page 26. Trim or not, depending on how you want to use the plant. Pinching back makes them bushier.

Variegated mint is a fabulous plant. This plant really likes instant containers so it may be one of our best trailers. Variegated mint will eventually trail 18 to 24 inches over the sides of a basket, but it takes a while. I've had it in the same basket for six months and it still looks fantastic.
Companions: I count on this foliage plant because it defines the colors around it and goes with almost anything. Use it with brighter colors, like brilliant reds, purples, and yellows in petunias, melampodium, or verbenas.

Growing Conditions

Season: Any frost-free season.
Light: Medium shade to full sun in cool weather. Medium to light shade in hot weather.
Water: Low.
Salt tolerance: Unknown.
Wind tolerance: Unknown.
Zone: Use as an annual.
Pest problems: Whiteflies.

Mona Lavender *(Plectranthus plepalila 'Mona Lavender')*

Characteristics and Care

Use: Centerpiece.
Growth rate: Medium.
Size: 16"-18" tall with about the same spread.
Colors: Light purple spiky flowers; dark green leaves with solid purple undersides.
Average life: 6 months.
Cautions: None known.
Care: Very easy. Fertilize on planting day with the slow-release mix described on page 26. I never trimmed mine.

Mona Lavender did very well in our container trials. Be sure to plant it in cool weather because it doesn't flower in hot summers. Mona Lavender required no maintenance at all once it was planted, other than watering.
Companions: This plant looks fabulous with other purples, like verbena, petunias, and lamium. Or, plant it with bright-colored flowers, like petunias and daisies.

Growing Conditions

Season: Thrives in temperatures from 36 to 80 degrees.
Light: Medium shade to full sun in cooler weather, but burns in the summer sun.
Water: Medium. We watered ours every third day.
Salt tolerance: Unknown.
Wind tolerance: Unknown.
Zone: Use as an annual.
Pest problems: We had no pests on ours.

Plant Profiles: The High Performers

Ornamental Kale or Cabbage *(Brassica oleracea)*

Characteristics and Care

Use: Edge or side. Too short to use as a centerpiece.

Growth rate: Medium.

Size: Low, about 4" to 6" tall.

Colors: Pink, purple, white, red.

Average life: 6 months.

Cautions: Unknown.

Care: Very easy. Fertilize on planting day with the slow-release mix described on page 26. I never trimmed mine.

Ornamental Cabbage did very well in our container trials. I had not expected it to thrive in the sides of containers, but it was outstanding performer! This cool weather plant thrived in temperatures from the low-20's to the mid-70's.

Companions: Use this plant with others that like the same temperatures. Pansies and violas are ideal.

Growing Conditions

Season: Prefers temperatures from the low-20's to the high 70's.

Light: Full sun to light shade.

Water: Medium.

Salt tolerance: Unknown.

Wind tolerance: Unknown.

Zone: Use as an annual.

Pest problems: We had no pests on ours.

Pansy *(Viola spp.)*

Characteristics and Care

Use: Mounding plants for sides and edges.

Growth rate: Medium.

Size: 4" to 6" tall by about 6" wide.

Colors: White, yellow, purple, brown, blue, pink, red and multicolors.

Average life: 4 to 6 months in containers.

Cautions: None known.

Care: Fertilize on planting day with the slow-release mix described on page 26. No trimming required, but they look better if you remove the dead blooms and leaves.

Pansies are just great for winter containers, where you can see the detail of those wonderful faces you often miss when they're planted in the garden. They don't have as much cold tolerance in instant containers as they do in the ground. And, they grow much slower than many of our summer plants, requiring more time to fill out the whole container.

Companions: Yellow pansies look great with red salvia and purple petunias in spring. Different colored pansies in the same container work well, too. Ornamental kale or cabbages are also great mates.

Growing Conditions

Season: Prefer temperatures from 20 degrees to 80 degrees. Don't look great at 20 degrees, but recover quickly when it warms up (see 'Zone', below).

Light: Light shade to full sun.

Water: Medium.

Salt tolerance: Medium.

Wind tolerance: Low.

Zone: Different varieties have different cold tolerance.

Pest problems: Occasional slugs or aphids.

Pentas, Butterfly *(Pentas lanceolata)*

Characteristics and Care

Use: Centerpiece.
Growth rate: Medium.
Size: 12 to 18 inches tall in containers.
Colors: Red, white, purple, or pink.
Average life: 3 to 5 months.
Cautions: None known.
Care: Fertilize on planting day with the slow-release mix described on page 26. Blooms more if dead flowers are removed.

Pink Butterfly Pentas   Red Butterfly Pentas

Pentas are great for heat tolerance and long bloom times. They are also one of the best plants for butterflies. However, they are quite confusing to buy because there are so many different kinds at the garden centers. Some do quite well, like the 'Butterfly Series', while others are short-lived, like the 'New Look' series. Ask the personnel at a reputable garden center for the best variety for your container. Be sure it will grow taller than your edge plants.
Companions: Use pentas with other flowering annuals that give a country garden look, like torenia and salvia.

Growing Conditions

Season: Any frost-free season. Takes high temperatures well.
Light: Light shade to full sun.
Water: Medium.
Salt tolerance: Medium.
Wind tolerance: Medium.
Zone: Grown all over the world as a summer annual. Frost sensitive.
Pest problems: Mites.

Persian Shield *(Strobilanthus dyeranus)*

Characteristics and Care

Use: Centerpiece.
Growth rate: Fast.
Size: In the top of a container, grows about 18" tall by 16" wide.
Colors: Purple.
Average life: 6 months.
Cautions: None known.
Care: Fertilize on planting day with the slow-release mix described on page 26. Give it room to grow because it grows very quickly. If it gets leggy, trim it hard because it will recover quickly.

Persian shield is a spectacular container plant. The leaves are so gorgeous they almost look artificial. Their iridescence gleams in arrangements. It works beautifully as a centerpiece, but don't try it in the sides. Although it grows well there, it sticks out awkwardly.
Companions: Use Persian shield with either bright colors or other shades of blue and purple.

Growing Conditions

Season: Does best in temperatures from 40 degrees to the mid-90's.
Light: Medium shade to full sun in the cooler weather; light to medium shade in temperatures over the low-90's.
Water: High.
Salt tolerance: Unknown.
Wind tolerance: Low.
Zone: Use as an annual.
Pest problems: We had none in our trials.

Plant Profiles: The High Performers

Petunia *(Petunia spp.)*

Characteristics and Care

Use: Mounding or trailing plant that works well along the edges. Tricky on the sides.
Growth rate: Medium.
Size: 6" to 18" tall.
Colors: Red, purples, white, yellow or pink.
Average life: 4 to 5 months.
Cautions: None known.
Care: Fertilize on planting day with the mix described on page 26. Apply a fungicide if the plant has spots on the leaves or wilts when the soil is moist. Remove dead blooms if you have the time!

Growing Conditions

Season: Different varieties take different temperatures. None take freezing weather.
Light: Full sun to light shade.
Water: Medium.
Salt tolerance: High.
Wind tolerance: High.
Zone: Use as an annual. Tolerant of light frost but not a freeze.
Pest Problems: Fungus and whiteflies.

Petunias are easy, very colorful, and a container classic. Some are small, clumping plants, and others cascade down the sides of a pot. However, hundreds of new cultivars are being sold. Some do well, others don't. Many died quickly in the sides our our containers. We had consistent success with 'Easy Wave' petunias, as well as Proven Winners' Supertunias .

Companions: Use with snapdragons, salvias, pansies and geraniums. They also look wonderful mixed with other colors of petunias.

Salvia, Annual *(Salvia spp.)*

Characteristics and Care

Use: Centerpiece
Growth rate: Medium.
Size: In the top of a container, the blue grows 15" to 18" tall. The red grows about 8" to 12" tall.
Colors: Many shades of white, red, peach, and purple.
Average life: 5 to 6 months.
Cautions: None known.
Care: Fertilize on planting day with the slow-release mix described on page 26. They flower more if you remove the dead blooms.

'Victoria Blue' Salvia

Annual Red Salvia

Growing Conditions

Season: Any frost-free season. Requires more maintenance in hot temperatures. The dead blooms need to be removed.
Light: Light shade to full sun.
Water: Medium.
Salt tolerance: Medium.
Wind tolerance: Medium
Zone: Used throughout the world as annuals.
Pest problems: I have never seen a pest on these plants but have heard of occasional thrips, mites, caterpillars, and slugs.

Annual salvias are some of the most useful centerpiece plants for instant containers. They not only bloom for five to six months without stopping but also offer spiky flowers. This vertical shape contrasts well with round flowers, adding textural interest to container arrangements. 'Victoria Blue' salvia is used as a perennial in many areas.

Companions: Use with round flowers like petunias and pansies. Add a cascading plant with small leaves and/or flowers, like creeping Jenny.

Shrimp Plant, Golden *(Pachystachys lutea)*

Characteristics and Care

Use: Centerpiece plant.
Growth rate: Fast.
Size: 1' to 2' tall.
Colors: Yellow.
Average life: 5 to 10 years in the ground in frost-free ares. A few months in a container.
Cautions: None known.
Care: Very easy. Fertilize every 6 to 9 months with the slow-release mix described on page 26. Be sure to underplant this plant with something full to cover the bottom stalks because they get leggy eventually.

Golden shrimp plants dependably bloom all the time for months on end, which is perfect for containers. The spiky shape of the flowers is also an excellent textural addition to many arrangements. And, this plant thrives in sun or shade. The golden shrimp is the highest performer of all the shrimp varieties on the market.

Companions: Use shrimp plants with other bright colors. It looks great with red and purple. I particularly like shrimp plants with pentas and coleus.

Growing Conditions

Season: Any frost-free season. Takes high temperatures beautifully.
Light: Medium shade to full sun. Happier with some break from noon sun in summer.
Water: Medium to high.
Salt tolerance: Medium.
Wind tolerance: Low.
Zone: 9 to 11. Use as an annual in other areas.
Pest problems: Caterpillars and snails.

Sweet Potato, 'Black Heart', Margarita, and 'Tricolor' *(Ipomoea batatas)*

Characteristics and Care

Use: Trailing plant.
Growth rate: Fast.
Size: They know no bounds...literally they'll shoot out ten feet!
Colors: Lime green, purplish-black, and pink.
Average life: 6 months.
Cautions: Poisonous if leaves are eaten.
Care: Fertilize every 6 to 9 months with the slow-release mix described on page 26. You will have to trim these to keep them from taking over your arrangement.

Sweet Potatoes are the best and the worst of plants. They are definitely the fastest growing trailing plant we have in this book. While that's an advantage, it's also a pain when they grow so fast they overtake other plants in the arrangement. But, the new color varieties are fabulous, definitely worth using. The 'Caroline' variety grows much slower than the rest, so it is easier to maintain. Plant them with snail bait because these are snail candy, and they'll look ragged in no time unless you protect them.

Companions: See the many arrangements in this book (Chapter 4) for lots of companion ideas.

Growing Conditions

Season: Any frost-free season.
Light: Medium shade to full sun.
Water: High.
Salt tolerance: Medium.
Wind tolerance: Medium.
Zone: Use as an annual.
Pest problems: Snails, snails, and more snails! Fungus, aphids, and white flies occasionally. I have given up on trying to spray this plant and just put up with small holes in the leaves.

Plant Profiles: The High Performers

Ti Plant *(Cordyline fructicosa)*

Characteristics and Care

Use: Centerpiece plant.
Growth rate: Medium.
Size: Varies by type. Most grow to about 2' tall in an instant container.
Colors: Shades of red, pink, and green.
Average life: 6 months in a container.
Cautions: None known.
Care: Fertilize on planting day with the slow-release mix described on page 26. The fertilizer should last from 6 to 9 months. Remove unsightly leaves throughout the year.

Ti Plants are one of the most useful centerpiece plants for container gardens. Their upright, spiky form contrasts well with round leaves and flowers. Ti plants are also easy to grow as long as you protect them from frost. They eventually develop trunk-like stems that are not attractive in containers, so be sure to underplant them with smaller plants to cover this up.
Companions: Use ti plants as the centerpiece of arrangements with a tropical look. They also work well with coleus and lime green plants, like sweet potato vine and creeping Jenny.

Growing Conditions

Season: Any frost free season. (See 'Zone')
Light: Medium shade to full sun, depending on variety.
Water: Medium.
Salt tolerance: Low.
Wind tolerance: Low.
Zone: Use as an annual unless you live in a frost-free area. The ti shown on pages 88-89 takes temperatures down to the mid-20's.
Pest problems: If holes appear in the leaves, it is probably snails.

Torenia, Trailing *(Torenia fournieri)*

Characteristics and Care

Use: Trailing plant for edges and sides.
Growth rate: Medium.
Size: Grows about 6" to 12" down the side of a container.
Colors: Shades of blue, purple, and red.
Average life: Up to one year with no frost.
Cautions: None known.
Care: Fertilize on planting day with the slow-release mix described on page 26. Trim off the tips if the plants become too large.

Torenia comes in either upright or trailing varieties. The trailing torenia is one of the top performers from our container trials. They are not only very easy to grow but also bloom all year in frost-free areas, even in the hottest parts of summer. The dark purple torenia (shown above, right) did the best in our trials, although all the colors did well.
Companions: Trailing torenia is one of the most useful container plants. Mix it with other shade of blue and purple for a monochromatic look. Or use bright reds and yellows to contrast with the blue and purples of the torenia.

Growing Conditions

Season: Any frost-free season.
Light: Light shade to full sun.
Water: Medium.
Salt tolerance: Medium.
Wind tolerance: Medium.
Zone: Tolerant of light frost but not a freeze.
Pest problems: None known.

Torenia, Upright *(Torenia fournieri)*

Characteristics and Care

Use: Mounding plant for edges and sides.
Growth rate: Medium.
Size: Mounds to about 8" tall and equally as wide.
Colors: Blue, pink, purple, white, red and multi. All have yellow centers.
Average life: 2 to 5 months in containers
Cautions: None known.
Care: Fertilize on planting day with the slow-release mix described on page 26. Trim back if it starts to droop. It takes about 2 to 3 weeks for it to recover a cutback.

Torenia thrived in our trials but they didn't last that long. They did great in the sides of the baskets, looking fabulous on planting day. However, they disappeared after 2 or 3 months. The other plants then filled in, so it was still a useful flowering plant.

Companions: Use wherever you need a small clump of color. I used the white torenia in all white arrangements, with caladiums and variegated mint. In summer, they look good with melampodium and pentas. They also look fabulous with coleus and dragon wing begonias.

Growing Conditions

Season: Prefer temperatures from about 50 to 95 degrees.
Light: Light shade to full sun.
Water: Medium. We watered ours every third day.
Salt tolerance: Medium.
Wind tolerance: Medium.
Zone: Summer annual in many parts of the world. Won't tolerate temperatures below 50 degrees.
Pest problems: Powdery mildew.

Viola *(Viola spp)*

Characteristics and Care

Use: Mounding plant for sides and edges.
Growth rate: Slow.
Size: 4 to 6 inches tall and equally as wide.
Colors: Lavender, blue, purple, red, brown and yellow.
Average life: 4 to 6 months.
Cautions: None known.
Care: Fertilize on planting day with the slow-release mix described on page 26. Deadhead for best blooming.

Violas are similar to pansies except the flowers are smaller. They do well during the coldest times of the years, and thrive in containers. Although they produce enough color to glow from a distance, the flowers are so detailed that I like to plant them in containers that I can see from a close distance.

Companions: Violas look great planted in mixed colors. They also look good mixed with other flowers, particularly in differing sizes. Alyssum is a good companion with smaller flowers and petunias are great choices for larger flowers.

Growing Conditions

Season: Prefer temperatures of 25 to 80 degrees.
Light: Medium shade to full sun in the cool season, but burns in the summer sun. Takes more shade than pansies.
Water: Medium.
Salt tolerance: Medium.
Wind tolerance: Medium
Zone: Use as an annual.
Pest problems: Occasional aphids or snails.

Other Plants That Deserve Mention: *Notes from our ongoing trials*

Lobularia maritima
Alyssum

This cool-weather plant looks great along the edge, but not on the sides of instant containers. Grow it in full sun in temperatures that range from 36 to 85 degrees.

Calibrachoa x hybridus
Calibrochoa

Resemble small petunias and do generally very well in containers. They did well along the edges but not in the sides in our trials. I still have a lot more varieties to test. Plant in sun and protect from freezes.

Bok choy
Chinese Mustard

Bok choy is a vegetable that makes a great transitional centerpiece between summer and winter. It grows will in sun, and requires trimming because it quickly outgrows its space.

Codaeium spp.
Crotons

Tropical shrubs that do very well in containers. Most of them take sun or shade and work well as centerpiece or edge plants. Sun or shade. Protect from frost.

Delphinium spp.
Delphinium

This plant is grown both as an annual and perennial. Many different types are available. I only tried the one shown above. It did quite well in full sun and cool (40 to 70 degree) temperatures.

Cineria spp.
Dusty Miller

An excellent annual - easy and dependable. Doesn't do well in the sides of instant containers, but thrives along the edges. Use in full sun in cooler temperatures.

Impatiens 'Little Lizzie'
Impatiens 'Little Lizzie'

A dwarf variety that deserves much more use in containers. Thrives both along the edges and in the sides of instant containers. Shares the same care needs as regular impatiens.

Alternanthera spp.
Jacob's Coat

An up-and-coming plant that I need a lot more experience with. The lime green type (shown) did not last long in the sides. I will work with more in the future.

Liriope spp.
Liriope, Monkey Grass

A tried-and-true plant for most areas of the world. Takes sun or shade. Works well as a centerpiece provided the edge plants don't grow taller than the liriope.

Lobelia spp.
Lobelia

One of my favorite container plants that has not been dependable in the sides of instant containers. Prefers cooler temperatures. I need to do a lot more work on this one!

Ophiopogon planiscapes 'Nigra'
Mondo Grass, Black

An unusual, expensive plant. Very tough. I only tried it in shade. Good for accents in avant garde arrangements.

Perilla magila
Perilla

A new-comer that resembles coleus. High performer as a centerpiece, in the sides, or along the edges of an instant container. Same care as coleus.

Catharanthus roseus
Periwinkle
White, pink, or purple flowers that do best in sun. Very heat-tolerant. Grow well in the sides and along the edges of instant containers, but stick out awkwardly.

Hypoestes phyllostachya
Polka Dot Plant
I tested this one because of its reputation for taking deep shade. It did alright, but not particularly well. In deep shade, it became leggy quickly.

Tradescantia pallida 'Purpurea'
Purple Queen
Although purple queen does well in the ground, I was not thrilled with its appearance in instant containers. It lived, but stuck out awkwardly.

Scaevola
Scaevola, Fan Flower
This plant did very well in full sun and high temperatures in the sides and along the edges of instant containers. Sadly, the ones we had planned to photograph for this book died in an unexpected freeze.

Schizanthus pinnatus
Schizanthus, Poor Man's Orchid
I really enjoyed working with this beautiful plant. It only lasted a month or two as an edge plant, but its label prepared me for its short life. Likes cool temperatures.

Antirrhimum majus
Snapdragon
Taller snapdragons did very well as centerpieces, although they didn't stay in bloom continuously. Smaller snapdragons did well on the edges but not in the sides of instant containers.

Acorus gramineus variegatus
Sweet Flag Grass, Dwarf Striped
Did very well in our trials as a centerpiece surrounded by <u>very</u> low edge plants (see page 32). Prefers light shade. Tolerates wet conditions. Grows to about 12" tall in a container. Zones 5 to 11.

Syngonium spp.
Syngonium, Nephitis
This trailing plant prefers shade and grows quite slowly. Behaves like a mounding plant for quite a while. Does well in the sides or along the edges of instant containers. Protect it from temperatures under 45 degrees.

Verbena spp.
Verbena
Upright verbena died quickly in the sides of instant containers. Trailing verbena did much better, but didn't bloom consistently. Prefers sun and warm temperatures.

Vinca major
Vinca Vine
One of my favorite trailers because it quickly grows long without taking over the other plants in the container. Does well along the edges or in the sides of instant containers. Shade.

Zinnia spp.
Zinnia
An excellent centerpiece plant for hot temperatures if you can find one that doesn't come down with fungus! Likes sun.

Bibliography

Armitage, Allan. *Armitage's Garden Annuals.* Portland, Oregon: Timber Press, 2004.

Crawford, Pamela. *Container Gardens for Florida.* Canton, Georgia: Color Garden Publishing. 2005.

Morton, Julia. *Plants Poisonous to People.* Miami, Florida: Hallmark Press. 1995.

Ross, Susan, and Schrader, Dennis. *Hot Plants for Cool Climates.* New York: Houghton Mifflin Company, 2000.

Smith, P. Allen. *Container Gardens.* New York, New York: Clarkson Potter/Publishers, 2005.

Williams, Paul. *Container Gardening.* New York, New York: DK Publishing, 2004.

Above: Wall pots are not only for walls! They work on swings, as well.

Index

Index

Video Series, Part 1: What is Side Planting?
(3 minutes)

Video Series, Part 2: Planting
(3 minutes)

Video Series, Part 3: Container Care
and Watering (3 minutes)

Video Series, Part 4: Fertilization and
Trimming (1.5 Minutes)

Video Series, Part 5: Wall Baskets and
Window Boxes (2.5 Minutes)

Video Series, Part 6: Patio Stands and
Border Columns (3.5 Minutes)